INFORMATION NOW

Information Now

Now

A Graphic Guide to Student Research

MATT UPSON,

C. MICHAEL HALL,

AND KEVIN CANNON

THE UNIVERSITY OF CHICAGO PRESS
CHICAGO AND LONDON

MATT UPSON IS ASSISTANT PROFESSOR AND DIRECTOR OF LIBRARY
UNDERGRADUATE SERVICES AT OKLAHOMA STATE UNIVERSITY.

C. MICHAEL HALL IS A WRITER, CARTOONIST, AND PUBLIC SPEAKER WHO ADVOCATES FOR COMICS AND
GRAPHIC NOVELS IN LIBRARIES AND EDUCATIONAL SETTINGS AND CREATES VISUAL AIDS FOR LIBRARIES.

KEVIN CANNON IS THE ILLUSTRATOR OF NUMEROUS EDUCATIONAL AND FICTIONAL GRAPHIC TEXTS, INCLUDING
UNDERSTANDING RHETORIC: A GRAPHIC GUIDE TO WRITING AND *THE CARTOON INTRODUCTION TO PHILOSOPHY.*

THE UNIVERSITY OF CHICAGO PRESS, CHICAGO 60637
THE UNIVERSITY OF CHICAGO PRESS, LTD., LONDON
© 2015 BY THE UNIVERSITY OF CHICAGO
ALL RIGHTS RESERVED. PUBLISHED 2015.
PRINTED IN THE UNITED STATES OF AMERICA
24 23 22 21 20 19 18 17 16 15   1 2 3 4 5

ISBN-13: 978-0-226-09569-1 (PAPER)
ISBN-13: 978-0-226-26775-3 (E-BOOK)
DOI: 10.7208/CHICAGO/9780226267753.001.0001

LIBRARY OF CONGRESS CATALOGING-IN-PUBLICATION DATA

UPSON, MATT, AUTHOR.
   INFORMATION NOW: A GRAPHIC GUIDE TO STUDENT RESEARCH / MATT UPSON, C. MICHAEL HALL, AND KEVIN
CANNON.
     PAGES CM
   ISBN 978-0-226-09569-1 (PBK.: ALK. PAPER) — ISBN 978-0-226-26775-3 (E-BOOK)   1. INFORMATION
LITERACY — COMIC BOOKS, STRIPS, ETC.   2. LIBRARY RESEARCH — COMIC BOOKS, STRIPS, ETC.   I. HALL, C.
MICHAEL, AUTHOR.   II. CANNON, KEVIN, AUTHOR.   III. TITLE.
   ZA3075.U67 2015
   025.5'24 — DC22015000685

⊗ THIS PAPER MEETS THE REQUIREMENTS OF ANSI/NISO Z39.48-1992 (PERMANENCE OF PAPER).

CONTENTS

PREFACE

This book has pictures, we swear! You just have to get past this enormous one-page chunk of text before you are rewarded with the ample fruits of your labor. OK, OK, take one quick sneak peek. Turn the page but come right back.

Great. Satisfied? Since we've got you here, there are two important items we want to address.

#1: This book is about information. How to find the right kind, how to use it effectively, how to evaluate it efficiently, etc. As a current or perhaps soon-to-be undergraduate, the information you use—and your understanding of it—is critical to your success as a student and as a future professional. We want this book to reinvent the way you think about information. We want you to be more critical of the information you find and use. We want you to have a better understanding of where the information you use comes from. We want you to be more aware of how to locate the best information for your needs. And we want you to realize that finding the best information can be hard work, *especially* now that there is more information being created by more people than ever before in human history. We want you to do a lot of things, but we're here to help. And when I say "we," I mean librarians. Obviously we're a little biased here, but librarians are one of the most important resources in your quest for information. We know our way around books. That's been our job for quite a while now. But more importantly, we're *information experts*. Books aren't our only tools; we're not limited to one medium. We know how to find stuff, and, more importantly, we can help you figure out how to find the right stuff on your own. So, if this book teaches you one thing (hopefully, it will teach you more, but . . .), it's that your friendly neighborhood librarian can and should be one of your first stops when you start researching. OK, enough self-promotion.

#2: We decided to make this book a comic because we believe that comics can more efficiently teach concepts and skills than traditional prose, thanks to their use of engaging combinations of text and images and appropriate utilization of metaphor and relevant context. Because comics stimulate the parts of your brain that handle visual elements as well as the parts that handle language, they can potentially give your brain more opportunities to connect with the content than you'd have with a strictly text-based book. Plus, comics are fun to write and draw and a *lot* more fun to read than your average textbook.

All right, we've said enough here. Read the book, learn something new, and enjoy!

INTRODUCTION

INTRODUCTION

INTRODUCTION

INTRODUCTION

CRITICAL THINKING EXERCISES

1. For the exercises in this book, create an online blog, website, Twitter feed (or any other type of online social media) that you can use to track your understanding of information literacy and the research process. Feel free to answer the questions by using text, images, video, sound, or any other approach, **BUT** be sure to use outside information ethically. (I know we haven't covered that yet, but for now, just be sure to let us know if you use information created by someone else and show us where you got it. When in doubt, **LINK**.) This can be formal or informal, but you should really focus on answering the questions honestly and thinking about your own understanding and experience finding and using information.

2. Have you ever experienced information overload when searching for information? Were you unable to make a decision because there was too much information or the information was inconsistent or conflicted? If so, think about and describe how you got into that mess in the first place. What kind of information were you looking for? How much time did you spend trying to find what you needed? Were you eventually successful, or did you give up and throw your computer in the trash? Can you think of any strategies you could have used to avoid the problem?

3. Is information overload a common problem for you, or are you confident in your ability to find and manage information?

4. If you are confident in your skills, explain why. Practice? Instinct? Luck? What makes your search skills so great? If you're not confident, how could you fix that?

CHAPTER ONE
THE PROCESS

Steps to Finding and Using the Right Information. Anytime. Anywhere.

NERVOUS YET? DON'T WORRY. WE'RE HERE TO HELP.

IN THIS CHAPTER, WE'LL DISCUSS HOW TO DIVE INTO THAT GIANT MESS OF INFORMATION AND UNEARTH WHAT YOU NEED TO CREATE SOMETHING COHERENT, STRUCTURED, AND USABLE. **RESEARCH** (IN THE LIBRARY OR ON THE WEB) IS THE PROCESS OF SEARCHING FOR, SELECTING, EVALUATING, AND USING INFORMATION TO MEET A NEED, ANSWER A QUESTION, OR RESOLVE A PROBLEM.

WE STUDY THE RESEARCH PROCESS MOSTLY FROM A CLASSROOM PERSPECTIVE, BUT YOU CAN APPLY THESE PRINCIPLES ANY TIME YOU NEED TO FIND AND USE INFORMATION. AND WHEN I SAY ANY TIME, I MEAN **ANY** TIME.

NOT ACCURATE

ha ha!

RESEARCH ISN'T SOMETHING TEACHERS, PROFESSORS, AND LIBRARIANS MAKE YOU DO JUST BECAUSE THEY LIKE SEEING YOU SUFFER...IT'S A SKILL SET WORTH LEARNING. THESE STEPS ARE USEFUL OUTSIDE THE CLASSROOM, IN THE WORKPLACE, AT HOME...EVERYWHERE!

for sale

WAAAAH!

IMAGINE YOUR BOSS NEEDS INFORMATION ON THE COMPETITION'S LATEST INNOVATION. HOW DO YOU GET IT? DOES THAT USED CAR YOU'RE LOOKING AT HAVE A GOOD SAFETY RECORD? WONDERING IF YOUR CHILD MIGHT NEED TO SEE A DOCTOR? HOW DO YOU FIGURE OUT WHAT INFORMATION IS SAFE TO USE?

THINKING CRITICALLY ABOUT INFORMATION CAN HELP IN THE CLASSROOM BUT, JUST AS IMPORTANTLY, ALSO HELP YOU THRIVE IN YOUR LIFE AND CAREER.

CHAPTER ONE

REGARDLESS OF WHAT APPROACH YOU TAKE, YOU'LL BEGIN WITH AN IDEA, A TOPIC.

PICK SOMETHING YOU'RE INTERESTED IN, SOMETHING YOU HAVE A **QUESTION** ABOUT. IF THE TOPIC IS ASSIGNED OR CHOSEN FOR YOU, APPROACH IT IN A WAY THAT'LL ALLOW YOU TO BE CREATIVE AND FIND THE INTERESTING ASPECTS OF THE TOPIC.

YOU'LL FIND THAT YOUR WORK WILL BE MUCH BETTER IF YOU'RE INTERESTED.

IF THE RESEARCH IS FOR A CLASS, BE SURE YOU KNOW WHAT'S EXPECTED FROM YOU. READ THE DETAILS OF THE ASSIGNMENT, AND ASK YOUR INSTRUCTOR FOR CLARIFICATION IF YOU'RE NOT SURE OF THE ASSIGNMENT'S PURPOSE. THAT PURPOSE WILL GUIDE YOUR RESEARCH.

IF, FOR EXAMPLE, YOU NEED TO WRITE AN ARGUMENT PAPER, YOU'LL HAVE TO FIND INFORMATION ON **BOTH** SIDES OF AN ISSUE.

AND BE SURE TO PLAN AHEAD. YOU MIGHT THINK YOU CAN GET AWAY WITH PUTTING THINGS OFF UNTIL THE LAST MINUTE, BUT THAT **WILL** BACKFIRE EVENTUALLY. YOU CAN NEVER ACCOUNT FOR EVERY POSSIBILITY.

WAIT UNTIL THE LAST MINUTE TO DO YOUR RESEARCH, AND EVENTUALLY THAT "LAST MINUTE" WILL BE THE DAY YOUR INTERNET GOES DOWN, OR THE LIBRARY GETS FUMIGATED, OR YOU BECOME THE FIRST FLU CASE OF THE SEASON.

NO SIGNAL

LIBRARY

CLOSED for FUMIGATION

JEEZ, WHAT ARE THE ODDS?

CRITICAL THINKING EXERCISES

1. How do you prefer to do research? Do you like to just "jump in" and see what information you come across? Or do you prefer to have more structure and develop your research methodically, from the ground up? Describe your normal process for developing a topic and finding information. What could you do to improve your own approach to the research process?

2. When searching online, how do you decide what information to look at and what information to ignore? How do you decide what is good or bad? Do you trust the search engine to provide you with the best information, or do you take steps to ensure that your search is designed to be effective?

3. Tell us about some research you've recently done. It doesn't have to be for academic purposes. Remember, research is about a question you've had and the process of answering it. You might have tried to find a good, new sci-fi book to read, or you might not have understood a pop culture reference from your favorite show. It could be anything. How did you attempt to find information to answer the question? Did you find more than one resource to help you? Did those resources disagree or conflict? If so, how did that affect your next steps and eventual answer?

4. The next time you research a topic, try keeping track of the resources you locate, regardless of where you find them or what format they take. As you read through each resource, note how your views on the topic change and explain how what you've learned will determine your next steps. Show your results to your instructor, a librarian, or even a friend, and get some feedback from them.

CHAPTER ONE

YOU NOW HAVE A TOPIC IN MIND AND A STRONG QUESTION TO GUIDE YOUR RESEARCH. BUT WHERE DO YOU START?

A GOOD PLACE TO BEGIN IS WITH SOME BACKGROUND INFORMATION. MANY LIBRARIES HAVE ENCYCLOPEDIAS IN PRINT OR DIGITAL FORMATS. ENCYCLOPEDIAS COVER **LOTS** OF TOPICS AND PROVIDE ENOUGH BACKGROUND INFORMATION TO HELP YOU IDENTIFY IMPORTANT **KEYWORDS**, OR TERMS YOU CAN USE LATER ON IN YOUR IN-DEPTH SEARCHING.

A B C D E F G

NOW, SOME INSTRUCTORS AND LIBRARIANS MIGHT SAY GOOGLE AND WIKIPEDIA ARE COMPLETELY OFF-LIMITS, BUT I DISAGREE.

THAT DOES **NOT** MEAN YOU SHOULD JUST DO A QUICK SEARCH WITH GOOGLE, COPY THE INFORMATION FROM THE WIKIPEDIA ARTICLE, AND SLAP YOUR NAME ON THE PAPER. THAT'S NOT COOL AT ALL.

Google

YOU'VE BEEN TOLD NOT TO USE THOSE RESOURCES FOR TWO REASONS:

#1 THE INFORMATION ON OPEN, USER-DRIVEN WEBSITES **CAN SOMETIMES** BE UNRELIABLE.

#2 YOU'VE PROBABLY BEEN USING WIKIPEDIA AND GOOGLE INCORRECTLY FOR ACADEMIC PURPOSES...THEY'RE **STARTING POINTS**, NOT THE **WHOLE SHEBANG**.

g W

GOOGLE IS A GREAT PLACE TO BEGIN A SEARCH FOR BACKGROUND INFORMATION. THE "PROBLEM" WITH GOOGLE IS THAT IT SEARCHES THROUGH A **VAST** AMOUNT OF INFORMATION, AND A LOT OF THE INFORMATION OUT THERE IS NOT USEFUL OR IS JUST PLAIN WRONG. SOME OF YOUR RESULTS WILL BE GREAT, AND MANY WILL BE OK, BUT TONS OF THEM WILL BE UTTER JUNK.

YOU CAN IMPROVE YOUR SEARCH RESULTS, AND WE'LL DISCUSS HOW LATER IN THE BOOK, BUT THIS IS WHY YOUR INSTRUCTORS MIGHT SAY: "DON'T GOOGLE!"

WIKIPEDIA IS PRETTY USEFUL AS YOUR FIRST EXPOSURE TO A TOPIC, BUT IT CAN BE UPDATED AND EDITED BY JUST ABOUT ANYONE. THIS CAN BE A REAL PROBLEM, ESPECIALLY WITH CONTROVERSIAL SUBJECTS. SOMETIMES PEOPLE TRY TO PROMOTE THEIR OWN VIEWPOINTS ON A TOPIC, AND THE FACTS GET BURIED UNDER BIASED OPINION!

THE WORLD'S BANKS ARE SECRETLY CONTROLLED BY **INTERDIMENSIONAL ALIENS!**

EVEN THOUGH WIKIPEDIA EDITORS TRY TO MAKE SURE EDITS ARE AS ACCURATE AND UNBIASED AS POSSIBLE, YOU SHOULDN'T USE IT AS A DIRECT SOURCE.

INSTEAD, USE IT TO GUIDE YOU TO OTHER, MORE RELIABLE RESOURCES. EVEN WIKIPEDIA SAYS THAT'S WHAT YOU SHOULD DO.*

AGAIN, WE'LL DISCUSS THIS MORE LATER ON.

*SEE en.wikipedia.org/wiki/ Wikipedia:Researching_with_Wikipedia.

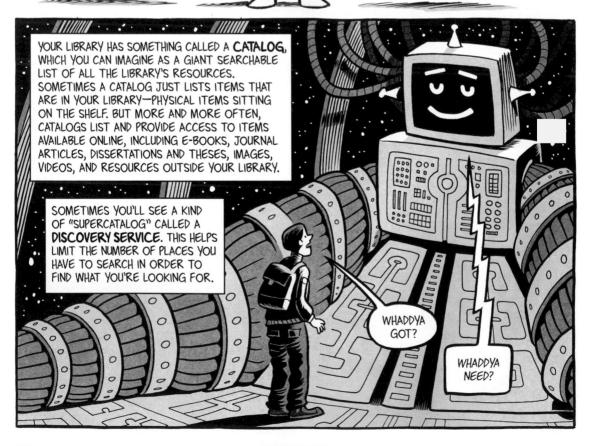

THE NEXT STEP IS TO GO FROM A GENERAL OVERVIEW OF A TOPIC TO A MORE IN-DEPTH LOOK.

BOOKS AND E-BOOKS ARE GREAT RESOURCES THAT CAN PROVIDE A LOT OF INFORMATION ON A TOPIC OR A PARTICULAR ASPECT OF THAT TOPIC. WHEN SEARCHING FOR BACKGROUND INFORMATION, YOU MIGHT COME ACROSS A **BIBLIOGRAPHY**, WHICH IS A LIST OF BOOKS AND OTHER RESOURCES ON A TOPIC. A BIBLIOGRAPHY THAT LISTS RESOURCES USEFUL TO YOUR RESEARCH CAN SAVE YOU A LOT OF TIME, BUT IF YOU DON'T FIND ONE, DON'T WORRY. WE CAN SEARCH FOR BOOKS IN OUR LIBRARY'S RESOURCES OR ONLINE.

Book

TABLET

YOUR LIBRARY HAS SOMETHING CALLED A **CATALOG**, WHICH YOU CAN IMAGINE AS A GIANT SEARCHABLE LIST OF ALL THE LIBRARY'S RESOURCES. SOMETIMES A CATALOG JUST LISTS ITEMS THAT ARE IN YOUR LIBRARY—PHYSICAL ITEMS SITTING ON THE SHELF. BUT MORE AND MORE OFTEN, CATALOGS LIST AND PROVIDE ACCESS TO ITEMS AVAILABLE ONLINE, INCLUDING E-BOOKS, JOURNAL ARTICLES, DISSERTATIONS AND THESES, IMAGES, VIDEOS, AND RESOURCES OUTSIDE YOUR LIBRARY.

SOMETIMES YOU'LL SEE A KIND OF "SUPERCATALOG" CALLED A **DISCOVERY SERVICE**. THIS HELPS LIMIT THE NUMBER OF PLACES YOU HAVE TO SEARCH IN ORDER TO FIND WHAT YOU'RE LOOKING FOR.

WHADDYA GOT?

WHADDYA NEED?

Fun to look at! But won't get you where you need to go.

Useful, relevant, ...and exactly what you need.

WITH THE ACADEMIC JOURNAL ARTICLES AND BOOKS FOUND THROUGH THE LIBRARY, YOU KNOW THAT, MOST OF THE TIME, YOU'RE GETTING SOME HIGH-QUALITY RESOURCES. STILL, SOMETHING IRRELEVANT CAN SLIP PAST EVERY ONCE IN A WHILE.

WHEN YOU USE GENERAL RESOURCES THAT YOU FIND ON THE INTERNET, THE LIKELIHOOD OF STUMBLING ON TO UNSUITABLE RESOURCES IS EVEN GREATER. AND SOMETIMES THE IRRELEVANT STUFF IS WHAT GETS PUSHED AT YOU FIRST.

AGAIN, I DON'T MEAN TO IMPLY THAT ALL INFORMATION FOUND ON THE OPEN WEB IS BAD. YOU JUST HAVE TO BE GOOD AT FIGURING OUT WHAT IS APPROPRIATE FOR YOUR NEEDS. PROFESSIONAL RESEARCHERS CAN JUST AS EASILY TWEET OR BLOG THEIR OWN OPINIONS AND RESEARCH AS YOU CAN. INFORMATION DOES NOT HAVE TO BE FOUND IN A BOOK OR A FANCY ACADEMIC JOURNAL TO BE VALID AND USEFUL.

MY LATEST RESEARCH CONCLUSIVELY PROVES THAT ELBOW PATCHES ON TWEED JACKETS WORN BY PROFESSORS SIGNIFICANTLY IMPROVE STUDENT ENGAGEMENT, ATTENTION, AND SUCCESS IN THE ACADEMIC CLASS... WAIT, 140-CHARACTER LIMIT... OK... **GOT THAT TWEED, Y'ALL!!!!!!**

snap!

GUESS WHO JUST DEVELOPED A **SWEET** PIEZOELECTRIC ROBOTIC ENDOSCOPE FOR COLONOSCOPY PROCEDURES? THIS GIRL!

TO ARM YOURSELF AGAINST THE ONSLAUGHT OF IRRELEVANT, INACCURATE, AND SOMETIMES INSIDIOUS INFORMATION ONLINE, YOU'LL WANT TO KEEP A FEW THINGS IN MIND.

YOU NEED TO KNOW WHO IS RESPONSIBLE FOR THAT INFORMATION.

Who created it?

Is it up-to-date? Does it help you answer your research question, or is it off-topic?

What is there to back up the author's conclusions?

Why was it written, and who was it written for?

Was it peer-reviewed?

ALL INFORMATION IS NOT CREATED EQUAL. YOU HAVE TO PUT IN SOME EFFORT TO ENSURE THAT YOUR RESEARCH IS GUIDED BY THE BEST, MOST RELIABLE, AND RELEVANT INFORMATION AVAILABLE.

THESE QUESTIONS ARE VERY IMPORTANT TO YOUR RESEARCH, AS WE'LL SOON SEE.

WHO? WHAT? WHY?

CHAPTER ONE

CRITICAL THINKING EXERCISES

REMEMBER TO USE YOUR ONLINE TOOL TO RECORD
YOUR RESPONSES TO THE QUESTIONS.

1. Take a closer look at your research question. Is it too broad or too specific? Often students have problems narrowing their question. Try to think about the different components in your question, and ask yourself if they can be broken down any further.

2. You might also try using something called a concept map to break down your question:

Try this out with your own topic, and see if you can develop a good research question or even multiple questions.

3. How do you find background information for your topic? How do you get started? Be honest, is it *Wikipedia*? Explain why you use a specific resource for background information, and share your thoughts on why that resource is the most useful for you. Do you use the information as a starting point, or do you use it as the core of your research? Which way is the correct way? (Hint: Reread the chapter!)

4. Try to find an expert on your topic. See who is writing academic articles on the topic, or search for a professional organization devoted to that topic. How do experts use the open Web to communicate? How are they using blogs, wikis, and social media to interact with

one another and the greater public? How is this information different than information you'd find in a book or a journal article?

5. Locate an academic resource on your topic, as well as a general online resource. For example, you might find a professional website on cancer treatment, as well as an online forum with public opinions on cancer treatment. How does the information in the two resources differ? How can you tell if one is "better" than the other? How do you know if you can trust the information in either resource?

CHAPTER TWO
HOW INFORMATION IS ORGANIZED AND FOUND
The Basics

FOR THIS DISCUSSION, I'M HANDING YOU OVER TO ANOTHER LIBRARIAN. SHE'S AN EXPERT IN THE ORGANIZATION OF INFORMATION AND FINDING THE RIGHT RESOURCES ONLINE AND IN LIBRARY CATALOGS AND DATABASES.

HI! I HEAR YOU'RE STARTING YOUR RESEARCH SOON! BUT FIRST, LET'S TALK ABOUT HOW INFORMATION CAN BE ORGANIZED, SO WE CAN FIND OUR WAY AROUND THE LIBRARY'S RESOURCES.

SEE YOU LATER!

YOU'RE GOING TO BE USING A LOT OF DIGITAL RESOURCES—AND WE'LL DISCUSS THAT SOON—BUT YOU NEED TO UNDERSTAND THE BASICS OF HOW PRINTED ITEMS ARE TYPICALLY ORGANIZED IN A LIBRARY.

OBVIOUSLY, WE HAVE A SHELF FULL OF BOOKS HERE, BUT HOW ARE THEY ARRANGED? RANDOMLY? A LOOSE ORGANIZATION BY SUBJECT OR TOPIC, KIND OF LIKE A BOOKSTORE? WELL, SINCE LIBRARIES CAN HAVE LITERALLY TONS OF BOOKS, WE KEEP THINGS AS STRUCTURED AND ORGANIZED AS POSSIBLE, SO FINDING MATERIALS IS EASY.

GEOLOGY

FOSSIL   VOLCANO   CRYSTAL

CLASSIFICATION IS THE METHOD WE USE TO KEEP OUR COLLECTIONS ORGANIZED. EACH ITEM IS DESIGNATED AS PART OF A SPECIFIC SUBJECT GROUP AND EVEN A SUBGROUP. FOR EXAMPLE, MOST OF THE BOOKS ON GEOLOGY WOULD BE GROUPED TOGETHER. WITHIN THAT GROUP WE FIND SUBGROUPS, LIKE PALEONTOLOGY, VOLCANOLOGY, AND MINERALOGY.

WHEN YOU SEARCH THE CATALOG FOR MATERIALS, YOU'LL SEE A **CALL NUMBER** FOR EACH ITEM. THAT'S JUST AN ALPHANUMERIC* TAG BASED ON THE ITEM'S SUBJECT. IT HELPS LIBRARIANS ORGANIZE SIMILAR ITEMS TOGETHER ON THE SHELF AND TELLS YOU WHERE TO LOOK WHEN SEARCHING FOR BOOKS. IT'S LIKE THE ADDRESS OF THE ITEM.

"VOLCANOES" 551.21 B891v

*THAT'S A FANCY WAY OF SAYING "LETTERS AND NUMBERS." BUT YOU KNEW THAT.

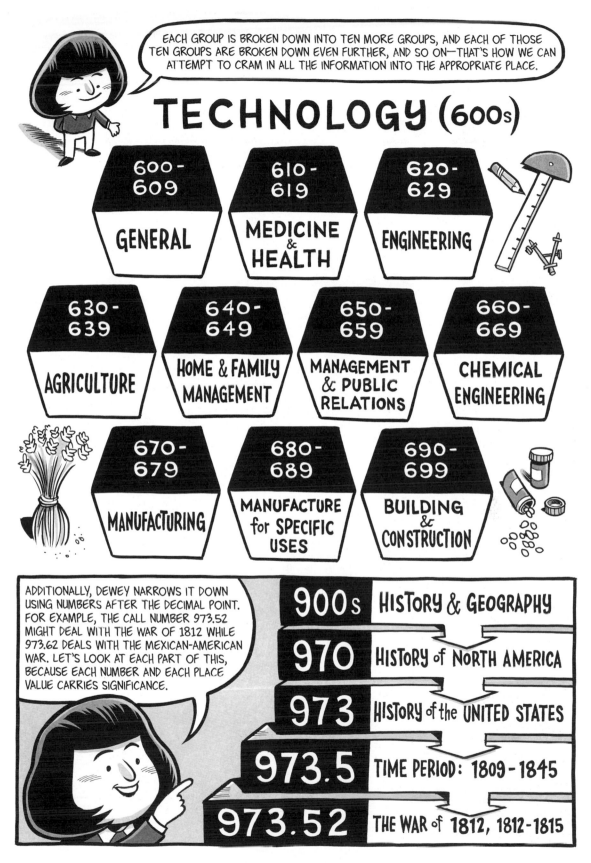

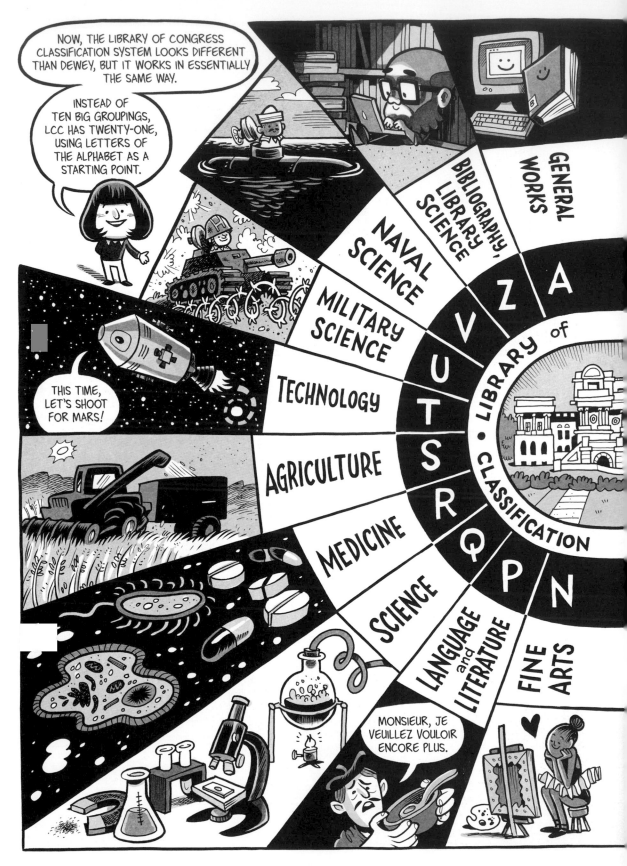

CHAPTER TWO

LCC BREAKS TOPICS DOWN WITHIN EACH LETTER, DIVIDING EACH LETTERED "CLASS" INTO "SUBCLASSES."

FOR INSTANCE, IN THIS BREAKDOWN, WE SEE THAT ITEMS ON SCULPTURE ARE FOUND UNDER NB, AND ITEMS ON PAINTING ARE FOUND UNDER ND.

CLASS N FINE ARTS

SUBCLASS N VISUAL ARTS

NA	ARCHITECTURE
NB	SCULPTURE
NC	DRAWING, DESIGN, ILLUSTRATION
ND	PAINTING
NE	PRINT MEDIA
NK	DECORATIVE ARTS
NX	ARTS IN GENERAL

FINALLY, LCC INSERTS A NUMBER AFTER THE CLASS/SUBCLASS TO CONTINUE TO NARROW THE FOCUS. BOOKS ON **VARMINT HUNTING*** CAN BE FOUND UNDER SK336.

CLASS S AGRICULTURE

SUBCLASS SK HUNTING SPORTS

SK336 VARMINT HUNTING

*AN ACTUAL TOPIC!

SOME LIBRARIES THROW IN A FEW NUMBERS AND LETTERS OF THEIR OWN AFTER THE "OFFICIAL" CALL NUMBER.*

THESE NUMBERS VARY BY LIBRARY AND CAN BE USED TO DESIGNATE THE TITLE, AUTHOR, OR PUBLICATION DATE OF THE BOOK...SOMETIMES EVEN ALL THREE. THIS IS JUST ANOTHER WAY TO REFINE CLASSIFICATION AND PROVIDE A UNIQUE CALL NUMBER FOR EVERY ITEM.

LCC

Varmint Hunting by Load N. Mygun

SK336 M373 v 1998

Call # | Author Last Name Code | First Letter of Title | Year of Publication

DDC

973.52 S337 W 2004

War of 1812 by Touch E. Subject

*THESE ARE ONLY EXAMPLES—YOUR LIBRARY MAY DIFFER.

320.973014 P253p 2012

THE REAL **WEAKNESS** OF THESE CLASSIFICATION SYSTEMS IS THAT WHEN NEW IDEAS COME ALONG—AND AT THE RATE TECHNOLOGY CHANGES, THAT'S PRETTY OFTEN—THE LIMITED SPACE IN THE SYSTEM GETS COMPRESSED. LONGER CALL NUMBERS HAVE TO BE ASSIGNED TO **SQUEEZE** EVERYTHING IN.

THESE SYSTEMS HAVE BEEN AROUND FOR AGES, AND IT'S STARTING TO SHOW.

HISTORY of the AMERICAS LCC CLASS E

WORLD HISTORY LCC CLASS D

THESE CLASSIFICATION SYSTEMS ORIGINATED IN THE UNITED STATES, SO THEY'RE KIND OF BIASED TOWARD AMERICAN AND WESTERN IDEAS. NOT AS MUCH SPACE WAS ASSIGNED TO NON-WESTERN MATERIALS, AND SO THEY MAY NOT BE REPRESENTED EFFICIENTLY.

NOW, ALL OF THAT TALK ABOUT HOW INFORMATION IS ORGANIZED IS PRETTY USELESS WITHOUT AN EFFECTIVE WAY TO SEARCH FOR THAT INFORMATION. BROWSING, WHETHER ON THE INTERNET OR IN PERSON, IS NOT THE MOST EFFICIENT WAY TO FIND EXACTLY WHAT YOU NEED. WHILE IT CAN SOMETIMES BE VERY SERENDIPITOUS, IT CAN ALSO BE UNFOCUSED AND HAPHAZARD.

TO MAXIMIZE THE USEFULNESS OF INFORMATION, WE NEED TO MAKE SURE YOU CAN FIND IT ON PURPOSE, NOT JUST HOPE YOU STUMBLE ACROSS IT BY BLIND LUCK.

MAYBE A COUPLE MORE LEFT TURNS...?

SO HERE COMES **METADATA** TO SAVE THE DAY!

METADATA IS INFORMATION ABOUT... INFORMATION. YEAH, IT'S THAT NERDY.

METADATA HELPS DESCRIBE THE INFORMATION IN A WAY THAT'S EASILY SEARCHABLE BY SYSTEMS LIKE DATABASES AND CATALOGS.*

*METADATA CAN HELP FIND INFO ON THE INTERNET TOO, BUT IT CAN BE LESS COMMON AND STANDARD-IZED THERE, ALTHOUGH THERE ARE EFFORTS TO MAKE THIS HAPPEN. SEARCH FOR INFO ON THE "SEMANTIC WEB" TO FIND OUT MORE.

METADATA CAN GET COMPLICATED, BUT HERE'S A SIMPLE EXAMPLE TO SHOW YOU HOW IT WORKS. HERE'S SOME INFORMATION ABOUT A CAR. EACH BIT OF INFORMATION MEANS SOMETHING, SO WE CAN DESCRIBE EACH PART WITH A LABEL.

METADATA ENABLES US TO PUT A SIGN ON A BIT OF INFORMATION EXPLAINING WHAT IT IS. THAT MIGHT NOT BE A BIG DEAL WHEN YOU'RE LOOKING AT JUST ONE ITEM, BUT WHEN YOU WANT TO SEARCH THROUGH HUNDREDS OR THOUSANDS OF RECORDS AND YOU WANT RESULTS THAT MEET ONLY CERTAIN CONDITIONS—CARS WITH UNDER 100,000 MILES OR UNDER $10,000—METADATA IS VITAL!

For sale:
2001 Talambro Lava, 84K, 4D, AC, CD, automatic, $8,250

For sale:
Model Year: 2001
Manufacturer: Talambro
Model: Lava
Mileage: 84,000 miles
# of doors: 4
Air-conditioning: yes
CD player: yes
Transmission type: automatic
Asking price: $8,250

WITHOUT ANY METADATA, OR WITHOUT A CONSISTENT SET OF METADATA, PERFORMING A GENERAL SEARCH OF THE WEB (AS OPPOSED TO LIBRARY RESOURCES OR AN ADVANCED ONLINE SEARCH) CAN RESULT IN A JUMBLE OF RESOURCES THAT CAN BE CONFUSING, MISLEADING, OR INCOMPLETE.

SEARCH RESULTS:

SOME METADATA WOULD'VE SPARED US THIS **INDIGNITY!**

SEARCHING THE INTERNET CAN BE MESSY.

ALTHOUGH GOOGLE HAS ADVANCED SEARCH OPTIONS ALLOWING FOR MORE OPTIMIZATION OF METADATA, MANY SITES LACK THE METADATA FOR SUCH SEARCHES. BESIDES, THE VAST MAJORITY OF US STILL JUST DO A GOOD OLD-FASHIONED, TRADITIONAL GOOGLE SEARCH ANYWAY... WE GO TO GOOGLE AND JUST START TYPING WHAT WE WANT OR HOPE TO FIND.

WHAT HAS BEEN SEEN CANNOT BE UNSEEN...

DUDE, WE HAVE **GOT** TO LEARN BETTER SEARCH TECHNIQUES.

A GENERAL SEARCH ESSENTIALLY LOOKS FOR YOUR SEARCH TERMS (OR KEYWORDS) WITHIN WEB PAGES RANKED BY GOOGLE. FOR EACH RESULT, THE PAGE IS RANKED ON WHERE AND HOW OFTEN THE PAGE USES A TERM, HOW MANY LINKS IT HAS, AND HOW LONG IT'S BEEN AROUND.*

CAN'T... STOP... LOOKING...

*THERE'S MORE TO IT, BUT THAT'S THE BASIC IDEA.

A GENERAL GOOGLE SEARCH IS LIKE GOING TO A GARAGE SALE AND RUMMAGING THROUGH BOXES FILLED AND LABELED IN A VERY GENERAL WAY. YOU MIGHT FIND A FEW GEMS HIDDEN IN THE BAGS AND BOXES, BUT THERE'LL ALSO BE LOTS OF IRRELEVANT OR USELESS MATERIAL. AND SOMETIMES THE VERY FIRST THING YOU PULL OUT WILL BE SO EXACTLY WHAT YOU'RE **NOT** WANTING, IT CAN THROW YOU OFF THE TRAIL ENTIRELY.

YOUR FINDINGS IMPROVE DRAMATICALLY WHEN YOU LEARN HOW TO SEARCH MORE EFFECTIVELY, AND IF THE INFORMATION IS DESCRIBED WITH A CONSISTENT SET OF METADATA!

BABY STUFF

CHAPTER TWO

DATABASES AND CATALOGS (WHICH ARE DESCRIBED IN MORE DETAIL LATER) ARE ONLINE LIBRARY RESOURCES THAT USE METADATA TO HELP MAKE SEARCHING EASY.

IMAGINE A HOUSE. THAT HOUSE IS LIKE A LIBRARY DATABASE OR CATALOG: IT CAN STORE ITEMS, JUST LIKE CATALOGS AND DATABASES STORE INFORMATION.

100 DATABASE PLACE

GARDEN HOSES

AUTO PARTS

FERTILIZER

AIR PUMPS

INSIDE THIS HOUSE, EVERYTHING IS WELL ORGANIZED AND LABELED, JUST LIKE A LIBRARY DATABASE OR CATALOG.

THESE LABELS ARE LIKE METADATA, DESCRIBING THE CONTENTS OF EACH CABINET.

HAND TOOLS

IN A LIBRARY RESOURCE, YOU WOULD SEE SOMETHING LIKE THIS. THIS IS ALL METADATA DESCRIBING A PARTICULAR ITEM. EACH LABEL REPRESENTS A DIFFERENT CHARACTERISTIC OF THAT ITEM.

PRINT | CITE | E-MAIL | SHARE

CATALOG

Title: *Evil Geniuses and the Superheroes Who Thwart Them: An Oral History*

Author: L. Luthor

Pages: 326 pages

Publisher: MetropoPress

Publication Date: 1940

Call #: 364.973 L884e

Subject Headings: Organized Crime—United States—History; Criminals; Superheroes; Crime—Prevention

Summary: For years, superheroes have prevented the dawn of a new age, an age dedicated to the consolidation of power under a few magnificent geniuses who have been unjustly labeled as "evil" or "mad." For the first time, the stories of these brave and unique "deviants" are offered in their own words.

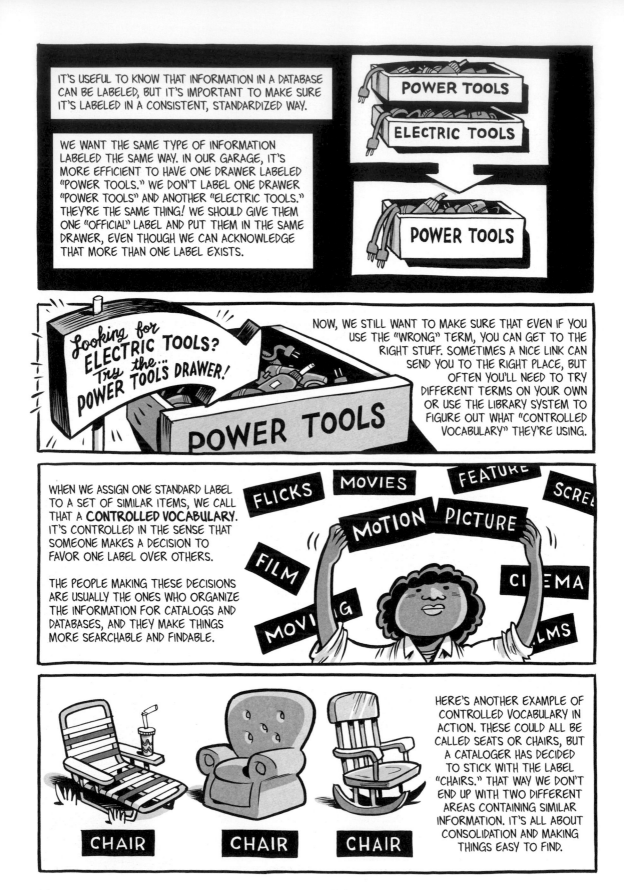

IT'S USEFUL TO KNOW THAT INFORMATION IN A DATABASE CAN BE LABELED, BUT IT'S IMPORTANT TO MAKE SURE IT'S LABELED IN A CONSISTENT, STANDARDIZED WAY.

WE WANT THE SAME TYPE OF INFORMATION LABELED THE SAME WAY. IN OUR GARAGE, IT'S MORE EFFICIENT TO HAVE ONE DRAWER LABELED "POWER TOOLS." WE DON'T LABEL ONE DRAWER "POWER TOOLS" AND ANOTHER "ELECTRIC TOOLS." THEY'RE THE SAME THING! WE SHOULD GIVE THEM ONE "OFFICIAL" LABEL AND PUT THEM IN THE SAME DRAWER, EVEN THOUGH WE CAN ACKNOWLEDGE THAT MORE THAN ONE LABEL EXISTS.

POWER TOOLS
ELECTRIC TOOLS
POWER TOOLS

Looking for ELECTRIC TOOLS? Try the... POWER TOOLS DRAWER!

POWER TOOLS

NOW, WE STILL WANT TO MAKE SURE THAT EVEN IF YOU USE THE "WRONG" TERM, YOU CAN GET TO THE RIGHT STUFF. SOMETIMES A NICE LINK CAN SEND YOU TO THE RIGHT PLACE, BUT OFTEN YOU'LL NEED TO TRY DIFFERENT TERMS ON YOUR OWN OR USE THE LIBRARY SYSTEM TO FIGURE OUT WHAT "CONTROLLED VOCABULARY" THEY'RE USING.

WHEN WE ASSIGN ONE STANDARD LABEL TO A SET OF SIMILAR ITEMS, WE CALL THAT A **CONTROLLED VOCABULARY.** IT'S CONTROLLED IN THE SENSE THAT SOMEONE MAKES A DECISION TO FAVOR ONE LABEL OVER OTHERS.

THE PEOPLE MAKING THESE DECISIONS ARE USUALLY THE ONES WHO ORGANIZE THE INFORMATION FOR CATALOGS AND DATABASES, AND THEY MAKE THINGS MORE SEARCHABLE AND FINDABLE.

FLICKS MOVIES FEATURE SCREE
MOTION PICTURE
FILM
MOVING
CINEMA
LMS

HERE'S ANOTHER EXAMPLE OF CONTROLLED VOCABULARY IN ACTION. THESE COULD ALL BE CALLED SEATS OR CHAIRS, BUT A CATALOGER HAS DECIDED TO STICK WITH THE LABEL "CHAIRS." THAT WAY WE DON'T END UP WITH TWO DIFFERENT AREAS CONTAINING SIMILAR INFORMATION. IT'S ALL ABOUT CONSOLIDATION AND MAKING THINGS EASY TO FIND.

CHAIR CHAIR CHAIR

SEAT OR CHAIR?

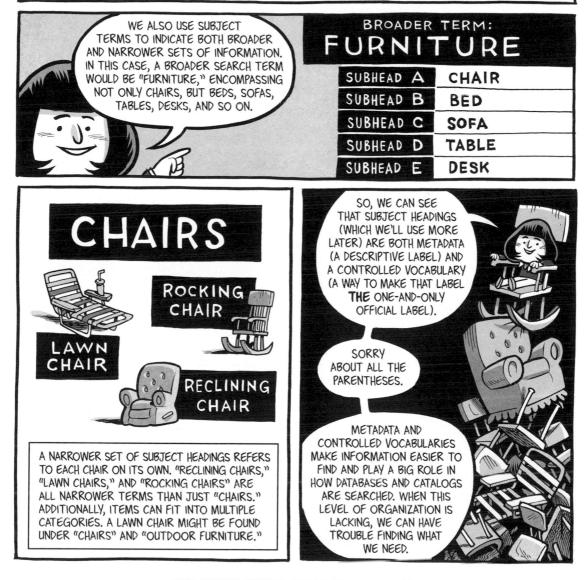

SUBJECT HEADINGS ARE A PARTICULARLY USEFUL KIND OF METADATA WITHIN DATABASES AND CATALOGS. REMEMBER THE CONTROLLED VOCABULARY WE JUST DISCUSSED? WELL, IN THIS CASE, THE SUBJECT HEADING IS "CHAIRS." IT COULD HAVE BEEN "SEATS," BUT OUR CATALOGER DECIDED THAT "CHAIRS" IS THE OFFICIAL TERM TO USE.

IF YOU SEARCHED FOR "SEATS" IN THIS CATALOG, YOU MIGHT SEE A MESSAGE LIKE "SEATS—SEE CHAIRS," WHICH LETS YOU KNOW YOUR TERM IS NOT THE PREFERRED OPTION WITHIN THE SYSTEM. LIBRARY RESOURCES ARE PICKY; IT CAN BE TOUGH TO FIGURE OUT HOW THEY WANT YOU TO SEARCH.

WE ALSO USE SUBJECT TERMS TO INDICATE BOTH BROADER AND NARROWER SETS OF INFORMATION. IN THIS CASE, A BROADER SEARCH TERM WOULD BE "FURNITURE," ENCOMPASSING NOT ONLY CHAIRS, BUT BEDS, SOFAS, TABLES, DESKS, AND SO ON.

BROADER TERM: FURNITURE

SUBHEAD A	CHAIR
SUBHEAD B	BED
SUBHEAD C	SOFA
SUBHEAD D	TABLE
SUBHEAD E	DESK

CHAIRS

LAWN CHAIR

ROCKING CHAIR

RECLINING CHAIR

A NARROWER SET OF SUBJECT HEADINGS REFERS TO EACH CHAIR ON ITS OWN. "RECLINING CHAIRS," "LAWN CHAIRS," AND "ROCKING CHAIRS" ARE ALL NARROWER TERMS THAN JUST "CHAIRS." ADDITIONALLY, ITEMS CAN FIT INTO MULTIPLE CATEGORIES. A LAWN CHAIR MIGHT BE FOUND UNDER "CHAIRS" AND "OUTDOOR FURNITURE."

SO, WE CAN SEE THAT SUBJECT HEADINGS (WHICH WE'LL USE MORE LATER) ARE BOTH METADATA (A DESCRIPTIVE LABEL) AND A CONTROLLED VOCABULARY (A WAY TO MAKE THAT LABEL **THE** ONE-AND-ONLY OFFICIAL LABEL).

SORRY ABOUT ALL THE PARENTHESES.

METADATA AND CONTROLLED VOCABULARIES MAKE INFORMATION EASIER TO FIND AND PLAY A BIG ROLE IN HOW DATABASES AND CATALOGS ARE SEARCHED. WHEN THIS LEVEL OF ORGANIZATION IS LACKING, WE CAN HAVE TROUBLE FINDING WHAT WE NEED.

CHAPTER TWO

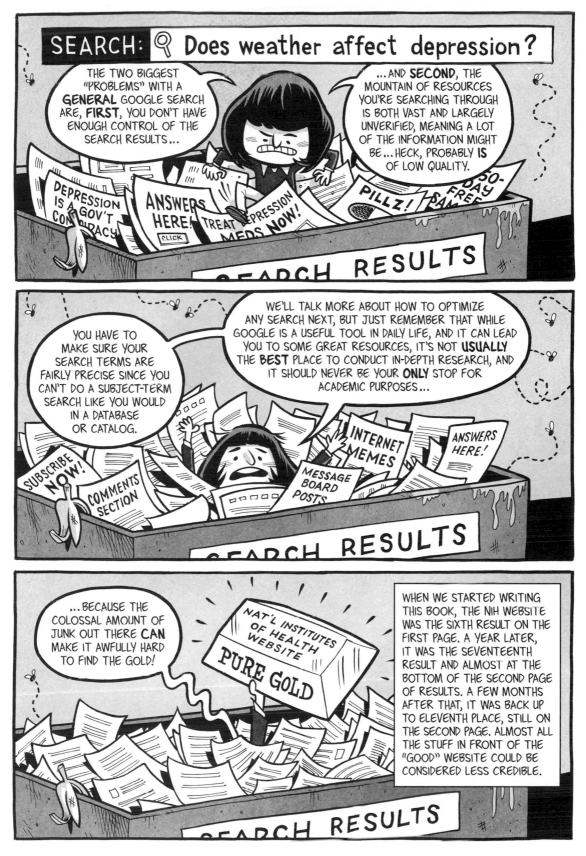

CRITICAL THINKING EXERCISES

REMEMBER TO USE YOUR ONLINE TOOL TO RECORD
YOUR RESPONSES TO THE QUESTIONS.

1. Which, if any, of the classification systems have you used? Dewey, Library of Congress, something else? Have you had success using the system? Why or why not?

2. Although these organizational systems attempt to keep up with social and technological changes, they are dated in many ways. What are some flaws that you can identify, and/or how can these systems be improved to enable accurate organization?

3. Perform a search in your library catalog for your topic (ask an instructor or a librarian for help if you need it). Once you find some results, look at the call number on a few of the items. Are the call numbers similar or not? If the call numbers are dramatically different, how do you explain that?

4. Perform a search for your topic in a library catalog or database. Find an item that interests you and click on it. This should take you to "the record." What kind of descriptive information (or metadata) do you see here? In other words, what kinds of details are provided about the item?

5. Perform a Google search for your topic. How many results did you get? Do the results look like they would be good for your academic research, or are they intended for a more broad audience? Try looking past the first page of results. What happens to the results as you page through? Do they become more or less relevant to your project? Can you see any difference in quality?

CHAPTER THREE
SEARCHING AND LIBRARY CATALOGS
Understanding the Hunt for Information

SO, WHERE DO WE FIND THAT INFORMATION "GOLD"? WELL, LIBRARY RESOURCES TYPICALLY PROVIDE THE BEST "GOOD" STUFF TO "BAD" STUFF RATIO. A LIBRARY CATALOG OR DATABASE LISTS ITEMS THAT ARE PROBABLY OF HIGHER QUALITY THAN MUCH OF WHAT WE'D FIND ONLINE, SO WE WADE THROUGH LESS GARBAGE.

OPEN WEB

LIBRARY RESOURCES

A QUICK POINTER:

REGARDLESS OF HOW OR WHERE YOU PERFORM A SEARCH, THE LIST OF ITEMS MATCHING YOUR SEARCH STATEMENT WILL LIKELY BE LONG... MULTIPLE PAGES, EVEN. DON'T JUST CLICK ON THE FIRST OPTION, ASSUMING IT'S THE BEST. THE SYSTEM HAS TO RANK YOUR RESULTS SOMEHOW, EVEN IF MULTIPLE ITEMS ARE AN "EXACT" MATCH FOR YOUR SEARCH TERMS. TAKE TIME TO SCROLL THROUGH THE LIST AND EXAMINE THE RESULTS!

SEARCH RESULTS

OBVIOUSLY, IT'S NOT LIKE THE RIGHT INFORMATION WILL JUST FALL IN YOUR LAP. YOU HAVE TO DO SOME WORK. YOU HAVE TO SEARCH.

BUT BEFORE YOU TRY OUT YOUR SEARCH SKILLS, I WANT TO EXPLAIN WHAT A **LIBRARY CATALOG** IS.

Title
Search Statements
Truncati
Boolean
Subj   t Ter
Oper
Author
Breadcrumb   Limi
Trail

Title: *Evil Geniuses and the Superheroes Who Thwart Them: An Oral History*

Author: L. Luthor

Pages: 326 pages

Availability: Central Library 2nd Floor and one e-book: *Click Here for e-Book*

Publisher: MetropoPress

Publication Date: 1940

Call #: 364.973 L884e

ISBN #: 978-X-368-44531-X

Subject Headings: Organized Crime—United States—History; Criminals; Superheroes; Crime—Prevention

Contents: Chapter titles include "Faster than a Speeding Meanie Pants," "Able to Destroy My Evil Plans in a Single Bound," "Criminals Are a Brave and Intelligent Lot," "With Great Power Comes Great Inability to Understand the Overarching Grand Design of My 'Schemes'"

Summary: For years, superheroes have prevented the dawn of a new age, an age dedicated to the consolidation of power under a few magnificent geniuses who have been unjustly labeled as "evil" or "mad." For the first time, the stories of these brave and unique "deviants" are offered in their own words.

Preview This Book link | Help | Cite/Export | Print | E-mail | Save | Share links

A KEYWORD SEARCH IS LIKE WALKING INTO OUR TRUSTY GARAGE HERE AND SAYING, "I NEED SOMETHING TO HELP ME DO YARD WORK," THEN SEARCHING THROUGH EACH AND EVERY DRAWER TO FIND EVERYTHING WITH ANY CONNECTION TO YARD WORK. YOU'LL FIND SOME STUFF THAT FITS YOUR (VAGUE) QUESTION, AND YOU'LL FIND SOME STUFF THAT COULD WORK BUT ISN'T REALLY WHAT YOU'RE LOOKING FOR, AND YOU'LL FIND A LOT OF STUFF THAT JUST WON'T WORK. YOU'VE SEARCHED THROUGH ALL THE RESOURCES, BUT YOU DIDN'T USE THE EXISTING ORGANIZATION TO FOCUS YOUR SEARCH ON THE RIGHT TOOLS.

U Search 🔍
Advanced Search

U Search ADVANCED SEARCH

All Fields ☑
• FULL TEXT
• SUBJECT
• AUTHOR
• TITLE
• CALL NUMBER
• SERIES TITLE
• JOURNAL TITLE

AND ▼
AND ▼
AND ▼
DATES: ☐ TO ☐

DON'T WORRY, THOUGH—WE CAN STEP UP TO AN **ADVANCED SEARCH** VIA A NUMBER OF OPTIONS AVAILABLE TO US IN CATALOGS AND DATABASES. YOU CAN USUALLY FIND A LINK CALLED "ADVANCED SEARCH" OR A DROP-DOWN MENU ALLOWING FOR MORE SEARCH OPTIONS. SELECT WHAT TYPE OF ADVANCED SEARCH YOU'D LIKE TO PERFORM. WE'LL TRY A SUBJECT SEARCH FIRST.

AS WE DISCUSSED PREVIOUSLY, CONTROLLED VOCABULARIES HELP US ORGANIZE INFORMATION BY USING A STANDARD LABEL FOR SIMILAR ITEMS. SUBJECT HEADINGS OR SUBJECT TERMS, WHICH ARE A TYPE OF CONTROLLED VOCABULARY, CAN ALSO HELP US **FIND** INFORMATION.

SEARCH RESULTS:

TITLE: *Evil Genius*
AUTHOR: L. Luthor
SUBJECT HEADINGS: Organized Crime—United States—History; Criminals; Superheroes; Crime—Prevention

WHEN I PERFORM A **SUBJECT SEARCH**, THE SYSTEM LOOKS THROUGH A LIST OF SPECIFIC LABELS ASSIGNED TO ITEMS, THEN PROVIDES ME WITH A LIST OF ITEMS MATCHING THAT LABEL. UNLIKE A KEYWORD SEARCH, A SUBJECT SEARCH JUST LOOKS THROUGH THE METADATA ASSOCIATED WITH SUBJECT TERMS, NOT THE **WHOLE** RECORD.

🌐 ACADEMIC WORLD SEARCH PLUS

comic books | SUBJECT TERMS ▼

• "Article Title"
Author Last Name, First Name. *Journal Title* volume #, issue # (Date): page range.
Subjects: **Comic books**, strips, etc.; Motion pictures and **comic books**

• "Article Title"
Author Last Name, First Name. *Journal Title* volume #, issue # (Date): page range.
Subjects: **Comic books**, strips, etc.; Horror **comic books**, strips, etc.

CHOOSE THIS OPTION TO JUST LOOK AT SUBJECT HEADINGS

LET'S GO BACK TO THE GARAGE. A **SUBJECT SEARCH** IS MUCH NEATER AND TIDIER THAN A KEYWORD SEARCH. IMAGINE THAT EACH DRAWER REQUIRES A KEY TO OPEN. THE RIGHT SUBJECT TERM ACTS AS THE KEY TO A SPECIFIC DRAWER: IT LETS US SELECT THE CORRECT ITEMS FROM A FOCUSED SET OF RESOURCES.

MANY ITEMS HAVE MORE THAN ONE SUBJECT TERM ASSOCIATED WITH THEM. FOR EXAMPLE, THIS SET OF ELECTRIC GARDEN SHEARS CAN BE LOCATED IN THE DRAWER FOR "GARDEN TOOLS" AND THE DRAWER FOR "POWER TOOLS." IT FITS INTO BOTH CATEGORIES AND CAN BE FOUND WITH A SEARCH FOR EITHER. THOSE WHO ORGANIZE THE INFORMATION ATTEMPT TO PROVIDE MORE THAN ONE WAY TO ACCESS WHAT YOU NEED.

BUT WHAT IF YOU DON'T KNOW THE LABELS THAT HAVE BEEN GIVEN? WHAT IF YOU'RE UNFAMILIAR WITH THE CORRECT SUBJECT HEADING FOR A TOPIC? THERE ARE A FEW OPTIONS TO GET ON THE RIGHT TRACK. USE A THESAURUS TO COME UP WITH ALTERNATE TERMS THAT MIGHT BROADEN OR NARROW YOUR SEARCH. OR USE A SUBJECT-TERM GUIDE PROVIDED BY YOUR CATALOG OR DATABASE, AND CHECK THE OFFICIAL SUBJECT TERM.

🔍 tools

Broader terms: ☐ HARDWARE
Narrower terms: ☐ AXES
☐ HAMMERS
☐ PLIERS
☐ SCREWDRIVERS
Related terms: ☐ EQUIPMENT

Title: *Evil Geniuses and the Superheroes Who Thwart Them: An Oral History*
Author: L. Luthor
Pages: 326 pages
Publisher: MetropoPress
Publication Date: 1940
Call #: 364.973 L884e
Subject Headings: Organize̶ ̶ ̶ ̶ited States—History; Criminals; Superheroes; Crime̶ ̶vention

CLICK HERE FOR ALL "SUPERHERO" RESOURCES IN ONE PLACE!

Summary: For years, superheroes have prevented the dawn of a new age, an age dedicated to the consolidation of power under a few magnificent geniuses who have been unjustly labeled as "evil" or "mad." For the first time, the stories of these brave and unique "deviants" are offered in their own words.

IF YOU'VE ALREADY FOUND A USEFUL ITEM THROUGH A KEYWORD SEARCH, LOOK AT THE SUBJECT TERMS LISTED IN THAT RECORD, THEN CLICK ON THE ONE THAT BEST MATCHES YOUR SEARCH. THAT'LL TAKE YOU TO A WHOLE LIST OF ITEMS MATCHING THAT SUBJECT HEADING!

AND REMEMBER THAT PEOPLE OR EVEN FICTIONAL CHARACTERS CAN BE **SUBJECTS**, TOO.

YOU CAN ALSO SEARCH BY AUTHOR.

TYPICALLY YOU PERFORM AN AUTHOR SEARCH BY PUTTING THE LAST NAME FIRST.* REMEMBER THAT SPELLING IS IMPORTANT—IF YOU MISSPELL THE AUTHOR'S NAME, YOU'LL END UP WITH A LIST OF AUTHORS FAR FROM YOUR INTENDED TARGET.

AUTHOR SEARCHES ARE GREAT FOR LOCATING **ALL** THE RESOURCES BY A PARTICULAR AUTHOR, WHICH COMES IN HANDY WHEN AN AUTHOR IS KNOWN FOR RESEARCH IN YOUR TOPIC AREA. WATCH OUT FOR AUTHORS WITH SIMILAR NAMES (MACCORMACK/ MCCORMICK) OR COMMON NAMES (WANG, HALL) SINCE THERE MIGHT BE A TON OF RESULTS!** AND YOU MIGHT WANT TO AVOID USING AN AUTHOR'S LAST NAME BY ITSELF...

OUTSIDE OF A DOG, A BOOK IS MAN'S BEST FRIEND. INSIDE OF A DOG, IT'S TOO DARK TO READ.

IN BOURGEOIS SOCIETY CAPITAL IS INDEPENDENT AND HAS INDIVIDUALITY, WHILE THE LIVING PERSON IS DEPENDENT AND HAS NO INDIVIDUALITY.

*YOU CAN ADD A COMMA BETWEEN THE NAMES, BUT MANY SYSTEMS FUNCTION WITHOUT IT.

**MANY AUTHOR HEADINGS NOTE AN AUTHOR'S DATES OF BIRTH AND DEATH; THIS WILL HELP YOU DISTINGUISH BETWEEN AUTHORS WITH THE SAME OR SIMILAR NAMES.

YOU CAN ALSO PERFORM SEARCHES BY TITLE.

OBVIOUSLY, THIS WORKS BEST WHEN YOU KNOW AN ITEM'S TITLE. IT MIGHT WORK WITH A CERTAIN PHRASE OR STRING OF WORDS FROM THE TITLE, BUT IF YOU'RE OFF, YOU MIGHT NOT FIND THAT ITEM. FOR EXAMPLE, I MIGHT REMEMBER THAT THE BOOK I WANT IS A SHERLOCK HOLMES STORY WITH A SCARY (SPOILER) "GHOST" DOG, SO I PERFORM A TITLE SEARCH FOR "SHERLOCK HOLMES."

THIS WOULD YIELD QUITE A FEW RESULTS, BUT SINCE THE TITLE OF THE BOOK IS ACTUALLY *THE HOUND OF THE BASKERVILLES* AND DOESN'T HAVE "SHERLOCK HOLMES" ANY-WHERE IN THE TITLE, I'D BE OUT OF LUCK. YOU MIGHT BE BETTER OFF WITH A KEYWORD OR SUB-JECT SEARCH IF YOU'RE NOT SURE ABOUT A TITLE.

OH, SURE, **HOLMES** IS THE STAR. IT'S NOT LIKE I'M **IN THE TITLE** OR ANYTHING...

WHEN IT COMES TO ADVANCED SEARCHING, JUST REMEMBER THAT WHEN YOU PERFORM AN AUTHOR, TITLE, OR SUBJECT SEARCH, THE SYSTEM JUST LOOKS THROUGH THOSE PARTICULAR HEADINGS, NOTHING ELSE.

USE THE RIGHT FIELD FOR YOUR SEARCH! AN AUTHOR SEARCH FOR "CIVIL WAR, U.S." WILL NOT RESULT IN WHAT YOU ARE HOPING TO FIND BECAUSE YOUR SEARCH TERMS WON'T BE LISTED WITHIN AN AUTHOR FIELD. MAKE SURE YOU KNOW WHAT TYPE OF SEARCH YOU ARE PERFORMING AND HOW TO INPUT YOUR TERMS.

YEAH, THAT'S THE SPOT...

ONE MORE THING TO NOTE: LIBRARY CATALOGS AND DATABASES ARE PRETTY PICKY ABOUT SPELLING,* SO MAKE SURE YOUR SEARCHES ARE SPELLED CORRECTLY, OR, IN THE CASE OF CERTAIN BOOK TITLES, SPELLED AS THE AUTHOR INTENDED. A SEARCH FOR "PET CEMETERY" MIGHT NOT FIND THE STEPHEN KING NOVEL *PET SEMATARY.* EVEN A KEYWORD SEARCH PROBABLY WON'T HELP YOU HERE.

COULD YOU BE MORE INSENSITIVE?

*THEY'RE GETTING BETTER, THOUGH.

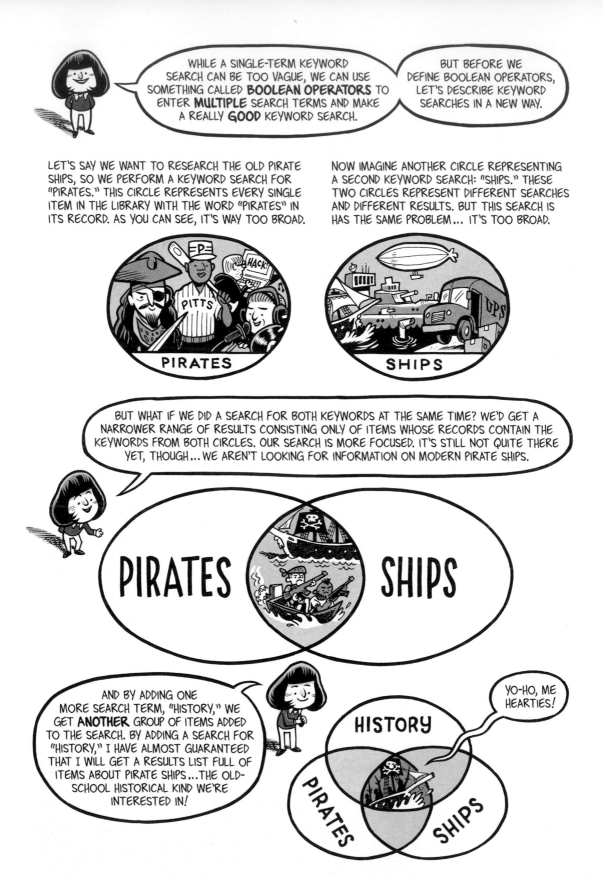

WHILE A SINGLE-TERM KEYWORD SEARCH CAN BE TOO VAGUE, WE CAN USE SOMETHING CALLED **BOOLEAN OPERATORS** TO ENTER **MULTIPLE** SEARCH TERMS AND MAKE A REALLY **GOOD** KEYWORD SEARCH.

BUT BEFORE WE DEFINE BOOLEAN OPERATORS, LET'S DESCRIBE KEYWORD SEARCHES IN A NEW WAY.

LET'S SAY WE WANT TO RESEARCH THE OLD PIRATE SHIPS, SO WE PERFORM A KEYWORD SEARCH FOR "PIRATES." THIS CIRCLE REPRESENTS EVERY SINGLE ITEM IN THE LIBRARY WITH THE WORD "PIRATES" IN ITS RECORD. AS YOU CAN SEE, IT'S WAY TOO BROAD.

NOW IMAGINE ANOTHER CIRCLE REPRESENTING A SECOND KEYWORD SEARCH: "SHIPS." THESE TWO CIRCLES REPRESENT DIFFERENT SEARCHES AND DIFFERENT RESULTS. BUT THIS SEARCH IS HAS THE SAME PROBLEM... IT'S TOO BROAD.

PIRATES

SHIPS

BUT WHAT IF WE DID A SEARCH FOR BOTH KEYWORDS AT THE SAME TIME? WE'D GET A NARROWER RANGE OF RESULTS CONSISTING ONLY OF ITEMS WHOSE RECORDS CONTAIN THE KEYWORDS FROM BOTH CIRCLES. OUR SEARCH IS MORE FOCUSED. IT'S STILL NOT QUITE THERE YET, THOUGH... WE AREN'T LOOKING FOR INFORMATION ON MODERN PIRATE SHIPS.

PIRATES   SHIPS

AND BY ADDING ONE MORE SEARCH TERM, "HISTORY," WE GET **ANOTHER** GROUP OF ITEMS ADDED TO THE SEARCH. BY ADDING A SEARCH FOR "HISTORY," I HAVE ALMOST GUARANTEED THAT I WILL GET A RESULTS LIST FULL OF ITEMS ABOUT PIRATE SHIPS...THE OLD-SCHOOL HISTORICAL KIND WE'RE INTERESTED IN!

HISTORY

PIRATES

SHIPS

YO-HO, ME HEARTIES!

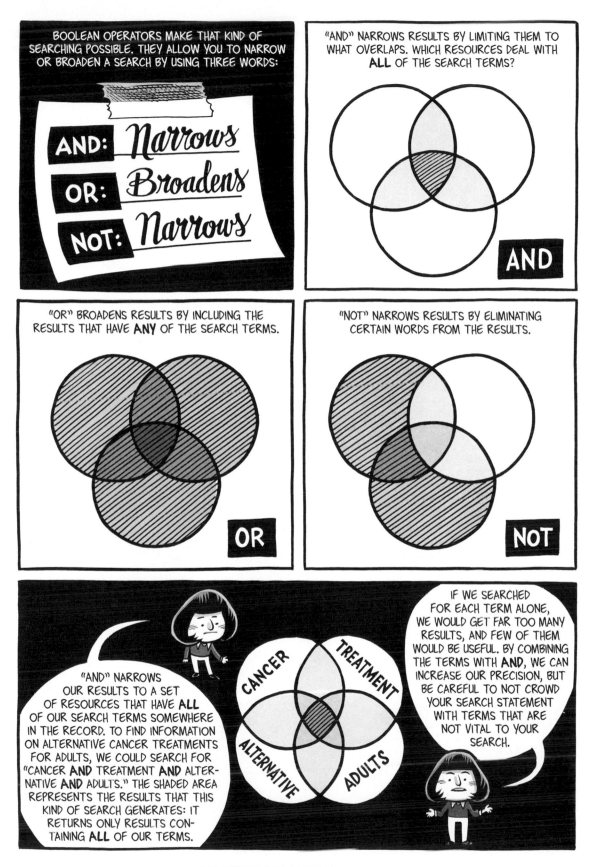

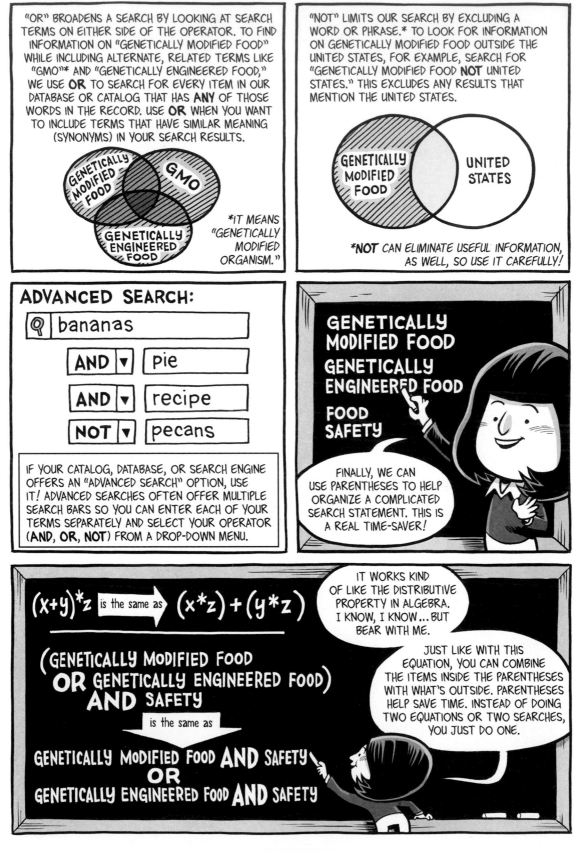

"OR" BROADENS A SEARCH BY LOOKING AT SEARCH TERMS ON EITHER SIDE OF THE OPERATOR. TO FIND INFORMATION ON "GENETICALLY MODIFIED FOOD" WHILE INCLUDING ALTERNATE, RELATED TERMS LIKE "GMO"* AND "GENETICALLY ENGINEERED FOOD," WE USE **OR** TO SEARCH FOR EVERY ITEM IN OUR DATABASE OR CATALOG THAT HAS **ANY** OF THOSE WORDS IN THE RECORD. USE **OR** WHEN YOU WANT TO INCLUDE TERMS THAT HAVE SIMILAR MEANING (SYNONYMS) IN YOUR SEARCH RESULTS.

GENETICALLY MODIFIED FOOD

GMO

GENETICALLY ENGINEERED FOOD

*IT MEANS "GENETICALLY MODIFIED ORGANISM."

"NOT" LIMITS OUR SEARCH BY EXCLUDING A WORD OR PHRASE.* TO LOOK FOR INFORMATION ON GENETICALLY MODIFIED FOOD OUTSIDE THE UNITED STATES, FOR EXAMPLE, SEARCH FOR "GENETICALLY MODIFIED FOOD **NOT** UNITED STATES." THIS EXCLUDES ANY RESULTS THAT MENTION THE UNITED STATES.

GENETICALLY MODIFIED FOOD

UNITED STATES

***NOT** CAN ELIMINATE USEFUL INFORMATION, AS WELL, SO USE IT CAREFULLY!*

ADVANCED SEARCH:

🔍 bananas

AND ▼ pie

AND ▼ recipe

NOT ▼ pecans

IF YOUR CATALOG, DATABASE, OR SEARCH ENGINE OFFERS AN "ADVANCED SEARCH" OPTION, USE IT! ADVANCED SEARCHES OFTEN OFFER MULTIPLE SEARCH BARS SO YOU CAN ENTER EACH OF YOUR TERMS SEPARATELY AND SELECT YOUR OPERATOR (**AND, OR, NOT**) FROM A DROP-DOWN MENU.

GENETICALLY MODIFIED FOOD
GENETICALLY ENGINEERED FOOD
FOOD SAFETY

FINALLY, WE CAN USE PARENTHESES TO HELP ORGANIZE A COMPLICATED SEARCH STATEMENT. THIS IS A REAL TIME-SAVER!

$(x+y)*z$ is the same as $(x*z)+(y*z)$

(GENETICALLY MODIFIED FOOD **OR** GENETICALLY ENGINEERED FOOD) **AND** SAFETY

is the same as

GENETICALLY MODIFIED FOOD **AND** SAFETY **OR** GENETICALLY ENGINEERED FOOD **AND** SAFETY

IT WORKS KIND OF LIKE THE DISTRIBUTIVE PROPERTY IN ALGEBRA. I KNOW, I KNOW...BUT BEAR WITH ME.

JUST LIKE WITH THIS EQUATION, YOU CAN COMBINE THE ITEMS INSIDE THE PARENTHESES WITH WHAT'S OUTSIDE. PARENTHESES HELP SAVE TIME. INSTEAD OF DOING TWO EQUATIONS OR TWO SEARCHES, YOU JUST DO ONE.

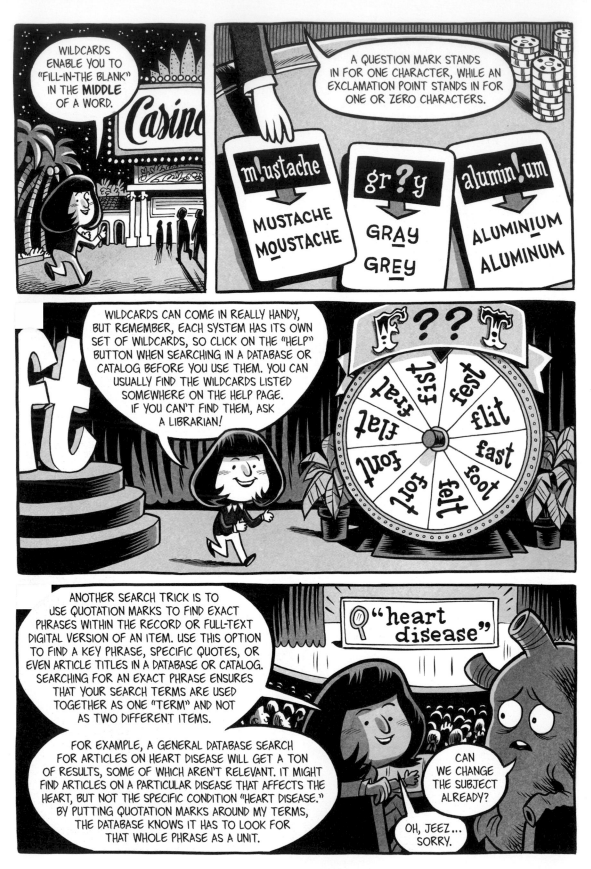

WILDCARDS ENABLE YOU TO "FILL-IN-THE BLANK" IN THE **MIDDLE** OF A WORD.

A QUESTION MARK STANDS IN FOR ONE CHARACTER, WHILE AN EXCLAMATION POINT STANDS IN FOR ONE OR ZERO CHARACTERS.

m!ustache → MUSTACHE M̲OUSTACHE

gr?y → GR̲A̲Y GR̲E̲Y

alumin!um → ALUMIN̲I̲UM ALUMIN̲UM

WILDCARDS CAN COME IN REALLY HANDY, BUT REMEMBER, EACH SYSTEM HAS ITS OWN SET OF WILDCARDS, SO CLICK ON THE "HELP" BUTTON WHEN SEARCHING IN A DATABASE OR CATALOG BEFORE YOU USE THEM. YOU CAN USUALLY FIND THE WILDCARDS LISTED SOMEWHERE ON THE HELP PAGE. IF YOU CAN'T FIND THEM, ASK A LIBRARIAN!

f ??? t

fest flit fast foot felt font flat frat fist

ANOTHER SEARCH TRICK IS TO USE QUOTATION MARKS TO FIND EXACT PHRASES WITHIN THE RECORD OR FULL-TEXT DIGITAL VERSION OF AN ITEM. USE THIS OPTION TO FIND A KEY PHRASE, SPECIFIC QUOTES, OR EVEN ARTICLE TITLES IN A DATABASE OR CATALOG. SEARCHING FOR AN EXACT PHRASE ENSURES THAT YOUR SEARCH TERMS ARE USED TOGETHER AS ONE "TERM" AND NOT AS TWO DIFFERENT ITEMS.

"heart disease"

FOR EXAMPLE, A GENERAL DATABASE SEARCH FOR ARTICLES ON HEART DISEASE WILL GET A TON OF RESULTS, SOME OF WHICH AREN'T RELEVANT. IT MIGHT FIND ARTICLES ON A PARTICULAR DISEASE THAT AFFECTS THE HEART, BUT NOT THE SPECIFIC CONDITION "HEART DISEASE." BY PUTTING QUOTATION MARKS AROUND MY TERMS, THE DATABASE KNOWS IT HAS TO LOOK FOR THAT WHOLE PHRASE AS A UNIT.

CAN WE CHANGE THE SUBJECT ALREADY?

OH, JEEZ... SORRY.

CRITICAL THINKING EXERCISES

1. Break down your research question or thesis statement into a few search terms. Now come up with a few synonyms or related terms for each one of your original search terms. Using Boolean operators and parentheses (if needed), take those terms and create a search statement that can be used in a library catalog or database search. Perform a search with your search statement. What are the results like? Did you find items that are appropriate? Are there enough resources or too many? How could you broaden or limit your results?

2. After locating some useful resources, take a closer look at the information in the records and list a few potentially useful subject headings. Try clicking on a few subject headings—what kinds of resources do you find?

3. Use the "help" option in your catalog and/or database. What kind of advanced search options are provided, and how do you use them? Which advanced search option do you find to be most helpful and why?

4. Which search terms worked best for you? Which did not work well?

5. Try doing a Google search for your topic, using your search statement. How do the results compare to what you saw in the library catalog and/or databases? How appropriate are the resources for your academic needs, and how far down the list did you have to go before you found something useful? Who is producing/creating the most useful information (this could be an individual or an organization), and how could you use that information to make your searching more efficient?

6. Access your library catalog, and try four different searches for "William Shakespeare": keyword, author, title, and subject. (Be sure to remember that subject and author searches may give you a list of specific headings that you will have to select before you get results.) How do your search results differ? How many results do you get for each search? How does a search for "Shakespeare, William" change the results of those searches? Explain why these searches offer different results. What type of results do you get with a Google search?

7. Perform an advanced search for your topic using Boolean operators (**AND, OR, NOT**). Note the number and type of results that are provided. Now try substituting some synonyms in for one or more of your search terms, and note how the results have shifted and if there

is any overlap with your first search. In other words, are your two different searches providing similar, if not identical results?

8. Feeling confident? Try a more complex search. Take the two searches you tried above and combine them. For example, I could take two searches—"gun **AND** laws" and "firearm **AND** laws"—and combine them into "(gun **OR** firearm) **AND** laws." Two searches for the price of one! How do those results compare with the first two searches?

CHAPTER FOUR
JOURNALS AND DATABASES

WE'VE TALKED ABOUT CATALOGS, SO LET'S TALK ABOUT THAT OTHER LIBRARY RESOURCE I KEEP MENTIONING: **DATABASES**. DATABASES ARE SIMILAR TO CATALOGS IN THAT THEY'RE SEARCHABLE COLLECTIONS OF INFORMATION. IN FACT, A CATALOG IS A KIND OF DATABASE.

WHEN WE USE THE TERM "DATABASE" IN A LIBRARY, THOUGH, WE'RE TALKING ABOUT A SYSTEM USED SPECIFICALLY TO ACCESS DIGITAL RESOURCES LIKE E-BOOKS, ENCYCLOPEDIA ARTICLES, IMAGES, COMPANY INFORMATION, AND ESPECIALLY ACADEMIC JOURNALS AND OTHER PERIODICALS.

AND **THAT** BRINGS US TO A VERY IMPORTANT QUESTION...

...WHAT ARE PERIODICALS AND JOURNALS?

FIRST OF ALL, A PERIODICAL IS SOMETHING THAT COMES OUT...**PERIODICALLY**. THAT EXPLAINS IT, HUH? PERIODICALS ARE ITEMS PRODUCED AND PUBLISHED EVERY DAY OR WEEK OR MONTH OR QUARTER OR YEAR AND SO ON. THEY CAN BE MAGAZINES, NEWS-PAPERS, AND ACADEMIC JOURNALS, WHETHER THEY ARE PUBLISHED ONLINE, IN PRINT, OR BOTH. UNLIKE BOOKS, WHICH ARE PUBLISHED ONCE AND HAVE FIXED CONTENTS (OTHER THAN NEW EDITIONS), PERIODI-CALS ARE AN ONGOING PROCESS OF GENERATING NEW CONTENT AND CONTINUAL PUBLICATION.

NAT'L TIMES

News Leak

Financial End Times

Basket Weaving Quart...

ALL CA... MONTH...

THOSE ARE IMAGINARY MAGAZINES, FOLKS.

POPULAR   **TRADE**   **SCHOLARLY**

PERIODICALS USUALLY FALL INTO ONE OF THREE CATEGORIES: POPULAR, TRADE/PROFESSIONAL, OR SCHOLARLY/ACADEMIC/PEER-REVIEWED. EACH CATEGORY HAS DISTINCTIVE CHARACTERISTICS YOU SHOULD REMEMBER WHEN PERFORMING ACADEMIC RESEARCH.

POPULAR RESOURCES ARE THE KINDS OF MAGAZINES AND NEWSPAPERS YOU SEE ON THE NEWSSTAND IN A BOOKSTORE OR GROCERY STORE, ALTHOUGH YOUR LIBRARY PROBABLY CARRIES MANY OF THEM AS WELL, EITHER ON THE SHELF OR IN ONLINE FORM.

POPULAR RESOURCES ATTRACT READERS WITH GLOSSY PAPER (IN PRINT), BRIGHT COLORS, IMAGES, EYE-CATCHING DESIGN, AND VIDEOS (ONLINE). THEY PROBABLY FEATURE LOTS OF ADVERTISEMENTS. NEWSPAPERS USE TOPICS OF LOCAL INTEREST TO APPEAL TO READERS.

POPULAR PUBLICATIONS ARE PUBLISHED FREQUENTLY; MONTHLY, WEEKLY, EVEN DAILY EDITIONS ARE COMMON. ONLINE PUBLICATIONS ARE UPDATED MULTIPLE TIMES DAILY. SEE, **CURRENCY** IS ONE OF THE MOST IMPORTANT FACTORS IN DETERMINING THE CONTENT IN POPULAR PUBLICATIONS, **OFTEN** AT THE EXPENSE OF ACCURACY. CURRENT ISSUES AND OPINION, NOT IN-DEPTH RESEARCH AND ANALYSIS, TEND TO MAKE UP THE BULK OF THESE PUBLICATIONS.

ARTICLES IN POPULAR PUBLICATIONS ARE WRITTEN BY JOURNALISTS FOR BROAD APPEAL—A PRIORITY FOR PUBLISHERS—BUT OCCASIONALLY AN EXPERT OR ACADEMIC CONTRIBUTES A "SPECIAL" ARTICLE. THE LANGUAGE USED IN POPULAR ARTICLES IS LIGHT ON JARGON AND RARELY VERY TECHNICAL, SINCE IT'S INTENDED FOR GENERAL AUDIENCES, AND ARTICLE TITLES ARE RELATIVELY STRAIGHTFORWARD.

POPULAR ARTICLES DON'T USUALLY CONTAIN CITATIONS OR REFERENCES THAT WOULD ALLOW A READER TO VERIFY THE RESEARCH OF THE AUTHOR. DEPENDING ON THE PUBLICATION, EDITORS MIGHT REVIEW THE ARTICLE AND CORRECT ANY POTENTIAL ERRORS BEFORE IT'S PUBLISHED.*

☐ COMPREHENSIVE?
☐ IMPARTIAL?
☐ VERIFIABLE?

BOTTOM LINE, POPULAR PERIODICAL ARTICLES CAN SUMMARIZE A CURRENT TOPIC OR OPINION, BUT THEY CAN'T GIVE YOU AN IN-DEPTH UNDERSTANDING OF AN ISSUE OR MUCH MATERIAL SUITABLE FOR AN ACADEMIC RESEARCH PROJECT.

*...AND THE EDITORS OF **SOME** POPULAR PUBLICATIONS AREN'T ALWAYS KNOWN FOR ACADEMIC IMPARTIALITY.

CHAPTER FOUR

PROFESSIONAL OR "TRADE" PUBLICATIONS SPECIALIZE IN INFORMATION RELEVANT TO A PROFESSION OR INDUSTRY, AND ARE OFTEN PUBLISHED BY A PROFESSIONAL ORGANIZATION. THEY FOCUS ON TRENDS AND NEWS IN THAT FIELD, GEARED TOWARD AN AUDIENCE FAMILIAR WITH THE PROFESSION'S UNIQUE TECHNICAL JARGON. YOU WON'T FIND ARTICLES AIMED AT A GENERAL READERSHIP. THE WRITERS AND EDITORS ASSUME THAT READERS HAVE SOME LEVEL OF PROFESSIONAL KNOWLEDGE. YOU MIGHT EVEN FIND SOME GREAT PROFESSIONAL INFORMATION ON A BLOG OR OTHER WEBSITE.

WHILE ORIGINAL RESEARCH IS NOT THE EMPHASIS OF A TRADE PUBLICATION, SELECT ARTICLES MAY BE RESEARCH-BASED AND PROVIDE CITATIONS AND REFERENCES. ARTICLES ARE USUALLY WRITTEN BY PROFESSIONALS IN THE FIELD OR STAFF WRITERS WITH KNOWLEDGE OF THE PROFESSION. SIMILAR TO POPULAR PUBLICATIONS, AN EDITOR HAS RESPONSIBILITY FOR ENSURING THAT ARTICLES ARE FORMATTED CORRECTLY PRIOR TO PUBLICATION AND ASSUMES SOME RESPONSIBILITY FOR ACCURACY, BUT THE ARTICLES ARE NOT NECESSARILY FACT-CHECKED.

ARTICLES FOUND IN TRADE PUBLICATIONS MAY BE SUITABLE FOR YOUR RESEARCH, BUT, AS WITH ANYTHING, YOU MAY NEED TO VERIFY QUESTIONABLE CLAIMS OR CONCLUSIONS.

TRADE PUBLICATIONS MAY USE SLICK DESIGN, EXCITING IMAGES, AND ADVERTISING. THEIR WEBSITES MAY ALSO BE COLORFUL AND EYE-CATCHING. THE TRICK TO DISTINGUISHING BETWEEN A PROFESSIONAL AND POPULAR PUBLICATION IS TO ASK SOME SIMPLE QUESTIONS:

"DO THE TITLES OF THE PUBLICATION AND THE ARTICLES INSIDE HIGHLIGHT THE INTENDED AUDIENCE OR PROFESSION? IS THERE A COMMON THEME? IS THE ADVERTISING RELATED TO THE CONTENT?"

TODAY'S TEACHER

Nurse News

OMOTIVE FERENCE UIDE

Free! EACHER the YEAR!

ROBOTICIST'S REPORT

MES

THE ADVERTISING IS A GOOD TIP-OFF. IN A TRADE PUBLICATION, YOU'LL SEE ADS FOR CONFERENCES, SUPPLIERS, OR OTHER PUBLICATIONS RELATED TO THE PROFESSION. UNLESS YOU'RE READING A SHAVING INDUSTRY MAGAZINE, YOU PROBABLY **WON'T** SEE AN AD FOR SHAVING CREAM.

TRADE PUBLICATIONS ARE USUALLY RELEASED IN PRINT FORM ON A MONTHLY OR BIMONTHLY BASIS, BUT LIKE POPULAR MAGAZINES, THEIR ONLINE VERSIONS MAY BE UPDATED MORE FREQUENTLY.

OK, NOW HOW EXACTLY DOES THIS RIVET GUN WORK...?

AND NOW, THE BIG ONE.

THE GOOD STUFF. THE **RESEARCH** GOLD MINE...

ACADEMIC JOURNALS. SCHOLARLY JOURNALS. PEER-REVIEWED JOURNALS. RESEARCH JOURNALS. ALL THESE NAMES REFER TO THE SAME THING: PUBLICATIONS WRITTEN BY PROFESSIONAL ACADEMICS AND RESEARCHERS, PUBLISHED BY PROFESSIONAL ORGANIZATIONS OR ACADEMIC INSTITUTIONS, AND FEATURING ORIGINAL RESEARCH AND ANALYSIS OF TOPICS IMPORTANT TO A PROFESSION OR ACADEMIC AREA. THESE JOURNALS PUBLISH SOME OF THE MOST CREDIBLE INFORMATION FOR A GIVEN FIELD. THE ACADEMIC JOURNAL ARTICLE IS ONE OF THE PRIMARY WAYS THAT SCHOLARS **COMMUNICATE** THEIR RESEARCH.

NOT ONLY DO ACADEMIC JOURNAL ARTICLES ALLOW SCHOLARS TO SHARE THEIR RESEARCH; THEY ALSO PROVIDE THE BASIS FOR THE RESEARCH OF OTHER SCHOLARS. RESEARCH IS A NEVER-ENDING PROCESS THAT'S DEPENDENT ON THE PREVIOUS WORK OF OTHERS. RESEARCHERS UTILIZE AND ACKNOWLEDGE THE WORK OF OTHERS IN THEIR OWN ENDEAVORS. IN THIS WAY, THE BODY OF RESEARCH CONTINUES TO GROW AND ADJUST AS NEW DISCOVERIES OR APPROACHES ARE FOUND. IMAGINE EACH RESEARCH ARTICLE AS A BRICK IN A BUILDING: IT'S SUPPORTED BY THOSE LAID BEFORE IT AND SUPPORTS THOSE COMING AFTER AND BUILDING ON TOP OF IT.

NATURALLY, ACADEMIC JOURNALS ARE AIMED AT A VERY PARTICULAR AUDIENCE CONSISTING OF PROFESSIONAL ACADEMICS AND RESEARCHERS, AND EMPLOY TECHNICAL OR DISCIPLINE-SPECIFIC JARGON. THE TITLE OF A JOURNAL USUALLY DESCRIBES ITS FOCUS AND OFTEN INCLUDES THE WORD "JOURNAL" TO MAKE SURE IT'S EASILY RECOGNIZED FOR WHAT IT IS. ARTICLE TITLES MAY BE **INTENSELY** SPECIFIC, JARGON-HEAVY, AND LONG. ARTICLES THEMSELVES TEND TO BE LONG, TOO, AND MAY FEATURE CHARTS, GRAPHS, TABLES, AND OTHER ILLUSTRATIONS SUPPORTING THE ARTICLE. YOU WON'T FIND ANY FLUFF OR MEANINGLESS IMAGES IN A JOURNAL ARTICLE.

YOU WON'T FIND ANY SHAVING CREAM ADS HERE, EITHER. IF THERE ARE ADS, THEY'RE FOCUSED ON SOMETHING SPECIFIC TO THE JOURNAL'S DISCIPLINE. YOU MAY SEE NOTICES FOR CONFERENCES OR OTHER PUBLICATIONS, MAYBE EVEN SPECIALIZED EQUIPMENT, TOOLS, OR RESOURCES USEFUL TO THE PROFESSION.

TRADITIONALLY, PRINTED VERSIONS OF ACADEMIC JOURNALS ARE STRAIGHTFORWARD, LACKING EMBELLISHMENT OR BRIGHT COLORS. YOU WON'T SEE A JOURNAL COVER FEATURING THE "WORLD'S HOTTEST VOLCANOLOGIST" ANYTIME SOON. WELL, ALL RIGHT, YOU **MIGHT** SEE THAT COVER, BUT "HOT" WON'T MEAN WHAT YOU'RE THINKING.

WHILE THERE ARE MANY, MANY, MANY ACADEMIC JOURNALS OUT THERE, YOU'LL PROBABLY SEE THEM ONLY IN YOUR LIBRARY OR A LIBRARY DATABASE. THEY CAN BE VERY EXPENSIVE* AND HAVE A LIMITED READERSHIP, SO YOU WON'T FIND THEM ON THE NEWSSTAND NEXT TO US WEEKLY.

...AND THE LATEST ISSUE OF THE JOURNAL OF CLINICAL ENDOCRINOLOGY AND METABOLISM? TRY NOT TO HAVE **TOO** MUCH FUN THIS WEEKEND.

*LIBRARIES SPEND A LOT OF MONEY ON JOURNALS. USE THEM! THAT'S WHAT THEY'RE THERE FOR!

STILL, THERE ARE MORE AND MORE "OPEN-ACCESS" ONLINE JOURNALS OFFERING FREE ACCESS TO ACADEMIC JOURNAL ARTICLES FOR USERS, AS OPPOSED TO THE OFTEN EXPENSIVE ONLINE JOURNALS AND DATABASES. WHILE OPEN-ACCESS JOURNALS CAN OFFER HIGH-QUALITY RESEARCH ARTICLES, SOME ARE NOT INDEXED, OR LISTED, IN TYPICAL LIBRARY DATABASES— BUT LIKE MOST THINGS, THAT'S CHANGING!

WHEN IN DOUBT, USE AN OUTSIDE RESOURCE LIKE THE DIRECTORY OF OPEN ACCESS JOURNALS IN ORDER TO SEARCH FOR CONTENT, AND, AS WITH ANY INFORMATION, DO YOUR BEST TO VERIFY THAT IT IS LEGITIMATE.

OPEN-ACCESS Club

• NO COVER CHARGE
• FREE PEER-REVIEW
• RESEARCH tonite!

VOLUME

TITLE VOL. 1 ISS. 1 | ITLE VOL. 1 ISS. 2 | ITLE VOL. 1 ISS. 3 | ITLE VOL. 1 ISS. 4 | ITLE VOL. 1 ISS. 5 | ITLE VOL. 1 ISS. 6

ACADEMIC JOURNALS, DEPENDING ON THE TITLE AND DISCIPLINE, ARE PUBLISHED MONTHLY, BIMONTHLY, QUARTERLY, ANNUALLY, OR EVEN ONLY ONCE EVERY FEW YEARS.

MOST OF THE TIME, JOURNALS HAVE A DESIGNATED **VOLUME** AND **ISSUE** NUMBER, EVEN IF THEY ARE **ONLY** PUBLISHED ONLINE. THE VOLUME NUMBER TYPICALLY REFERS TO THE WHOLE SET OF ISSUES PUBLISHED WITHIN A GIVEN TIME, USUALLY A YEAR, AND THE ISSUE NUMBER REFERS TO EACH INDIVIDUAL RELEASE.

FOR EXAMPLE, IF A JOURNAL IS PUBLISHED BIMONTHLY, THERE ARE A TOTAL OF SIX ISSUES EACH YEAR. THOSE SIX ISSUES ARE "CONTAINED" WITHIN ONE VOLUME.

NOT EVERY ISSUE WITHIN A VOLUME NUMBERS ITS PAGES STARTING FROM "1." JUST IMAGINE THE VOLUME IS ONE BIG COLLECTION BROKEN INTO A FEW SMALLER PARTS: THE PAGE NUMBERS IN ISSUE #1 START WITH "1," BUT ISSUES AFTER THAT MIGHT PICK UP WHERE THE PREVIOUS ISSUE LEFT OFF.

WHEN A NEW VOLUME STARTS, THE PAGE NUMBERS START OVER. IF A LIBRARY SUBSCRIBES TO HARD COPIES OF A JOURNAL, THEY MIGHT BIND ALL THE ISSUES IN A VOLUME TOGETHER INTO ONE BOOK-LIKE COLLECTION, KEEPING THE ENTIRE VOLUME TOGETHER AND MAKING IT MORE EASILY LOCATED ON THE SHELF.

THE AUTHORS OF JOURNAL ARTICLES ARE PROFESSIONAL SCHOLARS AND RESEARCHERS WHO WRITE TO SHARE THEIR RESEARCH OR ANALYSIS, OR TO COMMENT UPON OR **REVIEW** THE RESEARCH OF OTHERS. THE AUTHORS OF ACADEMIC ARTICLES ARE CAREFUL TO CITE THEIR RESEARCH AND PROVIDE COMPLETE REFERENCES SO OTHERS CAN VERIFY OR ATTEMPT TO DUPLICATE THEIR RESEARCH.

UNLIKE ARTICLES IN POPULAR AND TRADE PUBLICATIONS, MOST ACADEMIC JOURNAL ARTICLES GO THROUGH A PROCESS CALLED **PEER REVIEW**. THIS PROCESS HELPS ENSURE ACCURACY AND MAKES ACADEMIC ARTICLES IDEAL SOURCES FOR YOUR OWN RESEARCH.

I SHOULD CHECK THOSE REFERENCES AGAIN, I THINK...

WHEN AN ARTICLE IS PEER-REVIEWED, THE AUTHOR OF A PAPER SENDS IT TO THE EDITOR OF A JOURNAL. THAT EDITOR SENDS IT OUT TO OTHER EXPERTS WHO ARE QUALIFIED TO READ, EVALUATE, AND OFFER SUGGESTED CHANGES IN THE ARTICLE.

EDITORS SEEK OTHER VIEWPOINTS SO THAT THEY CAN DETERMINE WHETHER THERE IS A CONSENSUS OF OPINIONS ON THE PAPER. OFTEN THE NAMES OF THE AUTHOR(S) AND/OR OF THE REVIEWERS (AND OTHER IDENTIFYING ATTRIBUTES, SUCH AS UNIVERSITY AFFILIATION) ARE KEPT SECRET IN ORDER TO PREVENT PERSONAL BIAS FROM AFFECTING THE REVIEWERS' WORK.

THIS IS CALLED A **BLIND REVIEW**. THE PROCESS CAN TAKE MANY MONTHS, AND AUTHORS WILL LIKELY BE ASKED TO SUBMIT MULTIPLE REVISIONS THAT TAKE INTO ACCOUNT THE SUGGESTIONS OF THE REVIEWERS.

DATABASES, LIKE CATALOGS, ARE USED TO STORE AND RETRIEVE INFORMATION. IN FACT, A CATALOG **IS** A TYPE OF DATABASE. WE JUST DON'T CALL IT ONE, BECAUSE THAT WOULD BE CONFUSING... **MORE** CONFUSING.

THE REAL DIFFERENCE BETWEEN CATALOGS AND DATABASES IS THEIR PURPOSE. CATALOGS ARE MOST OFTEN USED TO LOCATE INFORMATION ON ITEMS HELD OR OWNED BY THE LIBRARY. LIBRARY DATABASES ARE USED TO LOCATE INFORMATION ABOUT ARTICLES OR TO LOCATE DIGITAL VERSIONS OF THE ARTICLES THEM-SELVES THAT THE LIBRARY DOESN'T NECESSARILY "OWN."*

DATABASES CAN DIG A LITTLE DEEPER THAN CATALOGS, TOO. YOU CAN USE A CATALOG TO FIND A JOURNAL, MAGAZINE, OR NEWSPAPER, BUT YOU CAN'T REALLY "OPEN" THOSE TITLES AND SEE THE ARTICLES INSIDE WITHOUT ACTUALLY WALKING TO A SHELF AND PICKING UP A COPY OF THE JOURNAL. A DATABASE ALLOWS YOU TO SEARCH WITHIN A SPECIFIC TITLE OR ACROSS MULTIPLE TITLES; THOUSANDS AND THOUSANDS OF TITLES CAN BE SEARCHED WITH ONE SET OF TERMS, SAVING YOU AN ENORMOUS AMOUNT OF RESEARCH TIME.

DATA-BASES

CATA-LOGS

AND EVEN IF YOU FIND AN ARTICLE THAT IS NOT ACCESSIBLE THROUGH THAT DATABASE, YOU CAN TRY TO FIND A HARD COPY OF IT IN YOUR LIBRARY OR REQUEST IT FROM ANOTHER LIBRARY. WHEN YOU'RE SEARCHING FOR ARTICLES, A DATABASE IS THE WAY TO GO.

ANOTHER DIFFERENCE BETWEEN LIBRARY CATALOGS AND DATABASES? THERE IS USUALLY ONLY ONE CATALOG FOR A LIBRARY, BUT IT'S LIKELY THAT THERE WILL BE MANY DATABASES. WHY SO MANY? WELL, THERE ARE A LOT OF ACADEMIC JOURNALS OUT THERE AIMED AT VERY SPECIFIC AUDIENCES. THERE ARE SOME VERY GOOD GENERAL DATABASES COVERING A LOT OF TOPICS, BUT THEY MIGHT LACK DEPTH; ON THE OTHER HAND, THERE ARE SUBJECT-SPECIFIC DATABASES COVERING A NARROW RANGE OF TOPICS, BUT PROVIDING A LOT OF DEPTH.

WHICH TYPE YOU CHOOSE DEPENDS ON YOUR RESEARCH NEEDS AND YOUR TOPIC. WHEN IN DOUBT, ASK A LIBRARIAN! THESE DATABASES CAN PROVIDE ACCESS TO SO MANY PUBLICATIONS, THAT YOU CAN EASILY GET LOST SEARCHING THROUGH THEM. YOUR LIBRARY MIGHT HAVE ACCESS TO OVER A HUNDRED DATABASES, EACH ONE COVERING A DIFFERENT TOPIC!

*REMEMBER THOSE DISCOVERY SERVICES THAT LOCATE BOTH PHYSICAL AND ELECTRONIC INFOR-MATION? THEY ARE ESPECIALLY USEFUL WHEN YOU WANT TO DO YOUR SEARCH IN ALL DISCIPLINES AND FIND MATERIALS IN ALL FORMATS SUCH AS BOOKS, JOURNAL ARTICLES, DISSERTATIONS, AND UNPUBLISHED WORKS. THE ONLY PROBLEM IS THAT YOU MIGHT BE OVERWHELMED WITH RESULTS.

CHAPTER FOUR

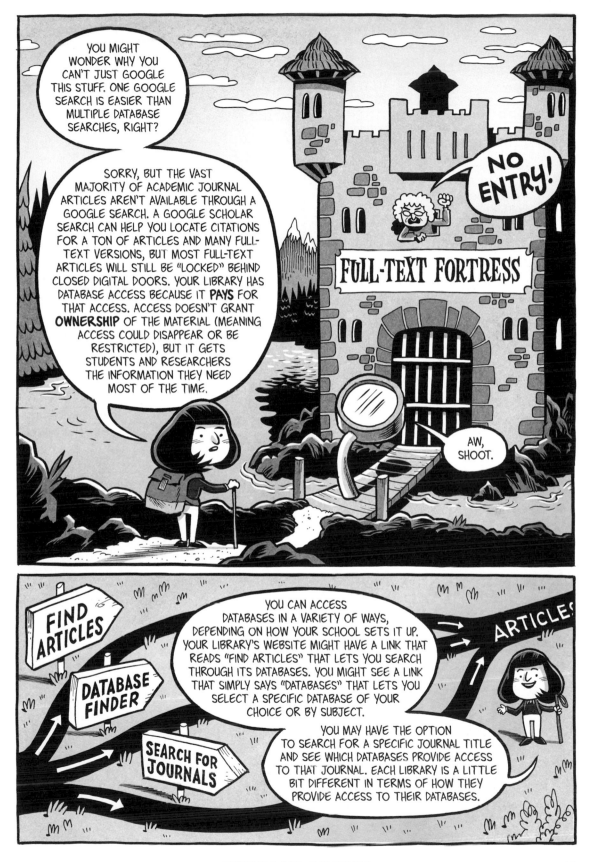

ACADEMIC WORLD SEARCH PLUS

SELECT A FIELD ▼

SEARCH MODE
⦿ Boolean
○ Find all
   search terms

TX – ALL TEXT
AU – AUTHOR
TI – TITLE
SU – SUBJECT
AB – ABSTRACT
PE – PEOPLE
PS – REVIEWS
IS – ISSN
IB – ISBN

DATABASES ARE SIMILAR TO CATALOGS WHEN IT COMES TO HOW THEY'RE SEARCHED. WHEN YOU PLUG IN SEARCH TERMS, THE SYSTEM LOOKS THROUGH THE METADATA TO FIND WHAT YOU'RE LOOKING FOR, JUST LIKE IN A CATALOG.

YOU CAN USE KEYWORDS OR DO AN ADVANCED SEARCH FOR TITLE, AUTHOR, OR SUBJECT, AMONG OTHER OPTIONS. YOU CAN ALSO USE BOOLEAN OPERATORS (**AND, OR, NOT**) BY INSERTING THEM INTO YOUR SEARCH OR BY USING THE DROP-DOWN OPTIONS.

WE WON'T REVIEW ALL THOSE SEARCH METHODS SINCE WE COVERED THEM EARLIER,* BUT I DO WANT TO HIGHLIGHT SOME ASPECTS UNIQUE TO DATABASE SEARCHES.

*EXCEPT FOR A FEW REMINDERS, BECAUSE YOU'RE AWESOME AND WE WANT YOU TO SUCCEED.

WHEN YOU PERFORM A SEARCH, YOU'LL GET A LIST OF RESULTS, SIMILAR TO WHAT YOU'D FIND IN A CATALOG... BUT THE INFORMATION WILL LOOK A BIT DIFFERENT. YOU'LL PROBABLY SEE THE ARTICLE TITLE ALONG WITH THE JOURNAL TITLE, VOLUME, ISSUE, AND PAGE NUMBERS, AND MAYBE A LINK FOR THE "FULL TEXT" OF THE ARTICLE.

ACADEMIC WORLD SEARCH PLUS

comic books | SUBJECT TERMS ▼

• "Article Title" *Click Here for Full Text*
Author Last Name, First Name. *Journal Title* volume #, issue # (Date): page range.
Subjects: **Comic books**, strips, etc.; Motion pictures and **comic books**

• "Article Title" *Click Here for Full Text*
Author Last Name, First Name. *Journal Title* volume #, issue # (Date): page range.
Subjects: **Comic books**, strips, etc.; Horror **comic books**, strips, etc.

PEER-REVIEWED SOURCES ONLY!

ALONGSIDE YOUR LISTED RESULTS, YOU'RE ALSO LIKELY TO BE GIVEN THE OPTION TO LIMIT OR "REFINE" YOUR SEARCH BY A VARIETY OF CRITERIA: "DATE," "RELATED SUBJECTS," "DOCUMENT TYPE" (ARTICLE, REVIEW, ESSAY, ETC.), AND "SOURCE TYPE" ARE ALL PRETTY COMMON.

TWO VERY IMPORTANT LIMITERS ARE THE "PEER-REVIEWED" LIMITER AND THE "FULL-TEXT" LIMITER. THE PEER-REVIEWED LIMITER (OR IT MIGHT SAY "SCHOLARLY" OR "ACADEMIC") WILL ELIMINATE A LOT OF THE RESULTS FROM YOUR LIST THAT DIDN'T GO THROUGH THAT PEER-REVIEW PROCESS WE TALKED ABOUT EARLIER.

LIMITING YOUR SEARCH THIS WAY GETS BETTER, STRONGER RESULTS, AND IT'S LIKELY THAT YOUR INSTRUCTORS WILL REQUIRE YOU TO USE ONLY THIS TYPE OF ARTICLE.

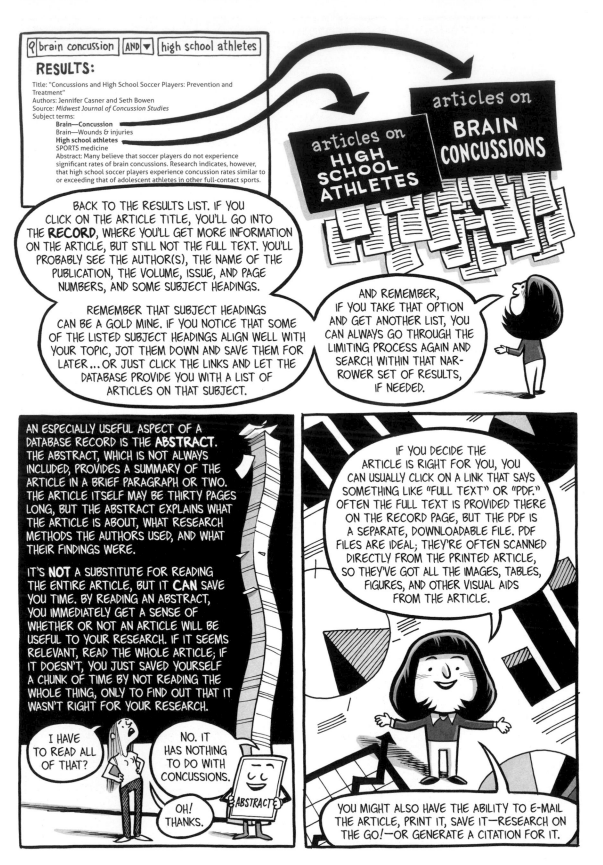

brain concussion AND ▼ high school athletes

RESULTS:

Title: "Concussions and High School Soccer Players: Prevention and Treatment"
Authors: Jennifer Casner and Seth Bowen
Source: *Midwest Journal of Concussion Studies*
Subject terms:
 Brain—Concussion
 Brain—Wounds & injuries
 High school athletes
 SPORTS medicine
Abstract: Many believe that soccer players do not experience significant rates of brain concussions. Research indicates, however, that high school soccer players experience concussion rates similar to or exceeding that of adolescent athletes in other full-contact sports.

articles on HIGH SCHOOL ATHLETES

articles on BRAIN CONCUSSIONS

BACK TO THE RESULTS LIST. IF YOU CLICK ON THE ARTICLE TITLE, YOU'LL GO INTO THE **RECORD**, WHERE YOU'LL GET MORE INFORMATION ON THE ARTICLE, BUT STILL NOT THE FULL TEXT. YOU'LL PROBABLY SEE THE AUTHOR(S), THE NAME OF THE PUBLICATION, THE VOLUME, ISSUE, AND PAGE NUMBERS, AND SOME SUBJECT HEADINGS.

REMEMBER THAT SUBJECT HEADINGS CAN BE A GOLD MINE. IF YOU NOTICE THAT SOME OF THE LISTED SUBJECT HEADINGS ALIGN WELL WITH YOUR TOPIC, JOT THEM DOWN AND SAVE THEM FOR LATER... OR JUST CLICK THE LINKS AND LET THE DATABASE PROVIDE YOU WITH A LIST OF ARTICLES ON THAT SUBJECT.

AND REMEMBER, IF YOU TAKE THAT OPTION AND GET ANOTHER LIST, YOU CAN ALWAYS GO THROUGH THE LIMITING PROCESS AGAIN AND SEARCH WITHIN THAT NARROWER SET OF RESULTS, IF NEEDED.

AN ESPECIALLY USEFUL ASPECT OF A DATABASE RECORD IS THE **ABSTRACT**. THE ABSTRACT, WHICH IS NOT ALWAYS INCLUDED, PROVIDES A SUMMARY OF THE ARTICLE IN A BRIEF PARAGRAPH OR TWO. THE ARTICLE ITSELF MAY BE THIRTY PAGES LONG, BUT THE ABSTRACT EXPLAINS WHAT THE ARTICLE IS ABOUT, WHAT RESEARCH METHODS THE AUTHORS USED, AND WHAT THEIR FINDINGS WERE.

IT'S **NOT** A SUBSTITUTE FOR READING THE ENTIRE ARTICLE, BUT IT **CAN** SAVE YOU TIME. BY READING AN ABSTRACT, YOU IMMEDIATELY GET A SENSE OF WHETHER OR NOT AN ARTICLE WILL BE USEFUL TO YOUR RESEARCH. IF IT SEEMS RELEVANT, READ THE WHOLE ARTICLE; IF IT DOESN'T, YOU JUST SAVED YOURSELF A CHUNK OF TIME BY NOT READING THE WHOLE THING, ONLY TO FIND OUT THAT IT WASN'T RIGHT FOR YOUR RESEARCH.

I HAVE TO READ ALL OF THAT?

NO. IT HAS NOTHING TO DO WITH CONCUSSIONS.

OH! THANKS.

ABSTRACT

IF YOU DECIDE THE ARTICLE IS RIGHT FOR YOU, YOU CAN USUALLY CLICK ON A LINK THAT SAYS SOMETHING LIKE "FULL TEXT" OR "PDF." OFTEN THE FULL TEXT IS PROVIDED THERE ON THE RECORD PAGE, BUT THE PDF IS A SEPARATE, DOWNLOADABLE FILE. PDF FILES ARE IDEAL; THEY'RE OFTEN SCANNED DIRECTLY FROM THE PRINTED ARTICLE, SO THEY'VE GOT ALL THE IMAGES, TABLES, FIGURES, AND OTHER VISUAL AIDS FROM THE ARTICLE.

YOU MIGHT ALSO HAVE THE ABILITY TO E-MAIL THE ARTICLE, PRINT IT, SAVE IT—RESEARCH ON THE GO!—OR GENERATE A CITATION FOR IT.

THAT BASICALLY EXPLAINS HOW TO PERFORM A SEARCH WITHIN A DATABASE. AGAIN, BE SURE TO USE A DATABASE RELEVANT TO YOUR TOPIC, AND USE A PRECISE, WELL-PLANNED SET OF SEARCH TERMS OR SEARCH STATEMENTS. IF YOU USE THE RIGHT COMBINATION OF SEARCH SKILLS AND THE APPROPRIATE DATABASE, YOU'LL FIND SOME EXCELLENT RESOURCES.

BUT WHAT IF YOUR INSTRUCTOR HAS GIVEN YOU A SPECIFIC ARTICLE THAT THEY WANT YOU TO LOCATE AND READ? THEY'VE GIVEN YOU THE CITATION, BUT THAT'S IT. NEW RESEARCHERS GET THIS KIND OF ASSIGNMENT ALL THE TIME. WHAT DO YOU DO?

ONE OPTION IS TO SEARCH THE CATALOG FOR THE JOURNAL TITLE AND TRACK DOWN THE RIGHT VOLUME AND ISSUE ON THE SHELF. ANOTHER OPTION IS TO SEE IF IT CAN BE FOUND IN ONE OF THE LIBRARY'S DATABASES.

CITATION DUDE

CATCH ME IF YOU CAN!

SINCE NOT EVERY JOURNAL IS INCLUDED IN EVERY DATABASE, IT'S USEFUL TO KNOW WHERE SPECIFIC JOURNALS ARE FOUND.

TRY LOOKING IN BOTH GENERAL AND SUBJECT-SPECIFIC DATABASES FOR THE JOURNAL TITLE. MOST DATABASES HAVE LINKS FOR SEARCHING THROUGH PUBLICATION TITLES; THEN NARROW YOUR SEARCH TO A SPECIFIC VOLUME, ISSUE, AND ARTICLE. YOU CAN ALSO TRY SEARCHING GOOGLE SCHOLAR TO FIND OUT WHICH DATABASES PROVIDE ACCESS TO A PARTICULAR JOURNAL.

MANY LIBRARIES HAVE A TOOL ON THEIR WEBSITES FOR SEARCHING FOR A SPECIFIC JOURNAL TITLE, BOTH IN PHYSICAL AND ELECTRONIC FORMAT. THESE TOOLS ARE GREAT. YOU CAN SEARCH FOR A JOURNAL TITLE AND GET A LIST OF ALL THE DATABASES CARRYING THAT JOURNAL. IF YOUR LIBRARY SUBSCRIBES TO THOSE DATABASES, YOU CAN JUST CLICK A LINK, JUMP DIRECTLY TO THE JOURNAL, AND START SEARCHING BY VOLUME, ISSUE, AND ARTICLE.

THE JOURNAL of SUPERHERO SCIENCE and CULTURE CAN BE FOUND IN:

OPEN-ACCESS JOURNALS DATABASE

SCIENCE JOURNALS ONLINE

ART AND CULTURE ONLINE LIBRARY

IF YOUR LIBRARY DOES HAVE A DISCOVERY SERVICE, YOU MAY SEE AN OPTION ON THE LIBRARY WEBSITE LABELED "FIND BOOKS, ARTICLES, AND MORE" OR SOMETHING SIMILAR. THIS SIMPLY ALLOWS YOU TO PLUG IN YOUR SEARCH TERMS OR ARTICLE TITLES, AND MULTIPLE DATABASES WILL BE SEARCHED FOR CONTENT. THIS CAN BE AN EASY OPTION, BUT IT ALSO MAY PROVE TO BE OVERWHELMING SINCE YOU'RE SEARCHING THROUGH A HUGE AMOUNT OF INFORMATION.

DISCOVERY SERVICE

Search

HUMANITIES DATABASE

SCIENCE DATABASE

LIBRARY CATALOG

LIBRARY ARCHIVES

SOCIAL SCIENCES DATABASE

ARTS DATABASE

JOURNALS AND DATABASES

ACADEMIC JOURNALS MIGHT ALSO OFFER BLOGS, PODCASTS, AND NEWS FOR FREE ON THEIR WEBSITES OR THROUGH SOCIAL MEDIA, SO IF YOU KNOW THAT THERE ARE SPECIFIC JOURNALS RELEVANT TO YOUR RESEARCH, BE SURE TO FOLLOW THEIR UPDATES. THIS INFORMATION CAN BE INCREDIBLY USEFUL, BUT UNLESS YOU KNOW TO LOOK FOR IT, IT MAY BE TOUGH TO FIND. JUST DO A GOOGLE SEARCH FOR THE JOURNAL OR SKIM THROUGH SUBJECT-SPECIFIC JOURNAL LISTS IN A DATABASE OR ON *WIKIPEDIA*.

IF YOU HAVE A CITATION YOU CAN'T LOCATE WITHIN A DATABASE, OR IF YOU FIND THAT YOUR LIBRARY DOESN'T HAVE FULL-TEXT ACCESS TO AN ARTICLE, YOU CAN REQUEST AN **INTERLIBRARY LOAN.** THIS IS THE PROCESS OF BORROWING AN ITEM FROM ANOTHER LIBRARY.

OFTEN, THESE **I.L.L.S** CAN BE INITIATED WITHIN A DATABASE. YOU MIGHT SEE A LINK THAT SAYS "I.L.L.," "FIND FULL TEXT," "BORROW FROM ANOTHER LIBRARY," OR SOMETHING ALONG THOSE LINES. THESE CAN HELP YOU USE YOUR LIBRARY'S SYSTEM TO REQUEST A COPY OF THAT ARTICLE.

EVEN IF YOU CAN'T DO THIS THROUGH THE DATABASE, YOUR LIBRARY WILL PROBABLY HAVE A REQUEST LINK ON ITS WEBSITE. TYPICALLY, THESE ARTICLES WILL BE MADE AVAILABLE DIGITALLY, MAKING THE LOAN PROCESS VERY EASY. YOU CAN ALSO DO THIS FOR BOOKS AND OTHER MEDIA, ALTHOUGH PHYSICAL ITEMS WILL HAVE TO BE SHIPPED TO YOUR LIBRARY.

I.L.L. (or the Magic Book Fairy)

YOU MEAN I HAVE TO HAUL THESE ALL THE WAY TO HAWAII?

LIBRARY

HERE, TAKE A LOAD OFF.

WHEN SEARCHING FOR ARTICLES, REMEMBER THERE ARE MANY DATABASES AND MANY WAYS TO ACCESS A JOURNAL OR AN ARTICLE. IT'S EASY TO GET FRUSTRATED, SO REMEMBER TO SPEAK WITH A LIBRARIAN WHENEVER YOU HAVE A QUESTION OR RUN INTO TROUBLE. AS I SAID, THERE'S **ALWAYS** A WAY TO GET THE INFORMATION YOU NEED. YOU JUST NEED THE RIGHT APPROACH.

WE COVERED A LOT OF GROUND IN THIS CHAPTER, AND YOU MIGHT BE FEELING A BIT OVERWHELMED. RELAX. IT TAKES WAY MORE ENERGY TO EXPLAIN THIS STUFF THAN IT DOES TO JUST PRACTICE IT YOURSELF.

ONCE YOU HAVE SOME EXPERIENCE WITH DATABASES, YOU'LL WONDER HOW YOU EVER GOT ALONG WITHOUT THEM!

INFO

EXIT

CRITICAL THINKING EXERCISES

1. How do you access databases at your institution? Are there multiple ways to access them? Examine your library's website or speak with a librarian in order to find out how, and then describe the process(es).

2. If your library has a list of databases (alphabetically or by subject), scan through and make a list of those that might be useful for your research. Remember that each database may offer different (and sometimes overlapping) material.

3. Pick two of those databases and see if you can locate a "help" link. Identify some specific advanced search options that are available through that database.

4. Perform a database search for your research topic in **two or more** databases, but don't limit the search to just peer-reviewed materials. Compare the results of the two searches. How do the results differ from each other? Look at your results and see if you can find examples of popular, trade/professional, and scholarly articles. List the examples and describe how you determined them to be popular, trade, or scholarly articles.

5. Use Google Scholar to find a citation for an academic article on your topic. Are you able to access the full text of that article? If not, what could you do to get the full text?

6. Use a database or Google Scholar to find an academic article on your topic. See what journal it is from. Use Google to search for the "official" site of the journal (it might be part of an organization or a larger publishing company). Describe "who" is responsible for publishing the journal, who the audience for the journal is, the stated purpose or scope of the journal, and what the submission guidelines and processes are. How does this information help ensure a high level of accuracy and reliability? Is the journal open access, or is a subscription required? Are there other features available on the journal website, like blogs, podcasts, and news updates? How might these other features be useful to your research?

7. See if you can find that journal listed in your library catalog, databases, or Discovery Service. If so, is the journal available in print in your library, digitally online, or both? How can you tell?

8. Find the *Directory of Open Access Journals* on the Web. Use the search option or browse to find a journal that could be potentially useful to your research. Determine and describe

what the article submission process is for that journal. How do these guidelines ensure high-quality research, and how do they compare to the submission requirements for a subscription journal?

9. If you have a citation for an article that can't be accessed through a Google search, how would you go about searching for that specific article in your library's resources? Keep in mind that your library may have hundreds of databases. Is there an easy way to hunt this down with only information on the author, title, journal, etc.?

CHAPTER FIVE

EACH SEARCH ENGINE FUNCTIONS A BIT DIFFERENTLY. STILL, THERE ARE BASIC STRATEGIES YOU CAN USE TO MAKE THE MOST OF A GENERAL WEB SEARCH. REMEMBER, SEARCHING THE WEB WILL DIFFER SOME FROM SEARCHING A LIBRARY DATABASE BOTH IN TERMS OF RESULTS **AND** SEARCH TECHNIQUE.

MAKE SURE YOUR GENERAL WEB SEARCH IS PRECISE AND CONTAINS MULTIPLE RELEVANT TERMS.* FORMULATE YOUR SEARCH TERMS CAREFULLY, AND DON'T WASTE TIME WITH FLUFF WORDS THAT DON'T HELP SPECIFY WHAT YOU'RE LOOKING FOR.

SEARCH TIME

high school soccer concussion prevention

*LUCKILY, YOU'VE ALREADY MASTERED THOSE SKILLS!

SEARCH ENGINES ALSO HAVE **ADVANCED SEARCHING** OPTIONS, BUT THEY'RE NOT QUITE LIKE THOSE FOUND IN CATALOGS AND DATABASES.

FOR ONE THING, THE ADVANCED SEARCH OPTION MIGHT BE TOUGH TO FIND. WITH GOOGLE, YOU HAVE TO EITHER SEARCH FOR "ADVANCED SEARCH" OR SEARCH FOR YOUR TERMS, **THEN** LOCATE THE ADVANCED SEARCH LINK AT THE BOTTOM OF THE PAGE.

TIME   ADVANCED SEARCH

ONCE YOU'VE FOUND IT, YOU'LL SEE THE ADVANCED SEARCH LACKS SUBJECT, AUTHOR, OR TITLE SEARCH OPTIONS. YOU **WILL** BE ABLE TO LIMIT OR EXPAND YOUR SEARCH A FEW DIFFERENT WAYS, HOWEVER.

YOU CAN ESSENTIALLY REPLICATE BOOLEAN LIMITERS (**AND, OR, NOT**) BY USING ADVANCED SEARCH OPTIONS.

YOU MIGHT BE OFFERED MULTIPLE SEARCH BARS. ONE MIGHT SEARCH FOR "ALL THESE WORDS," WHICH IS SIMILAR TO AN "**AND**" SEARCH.

A BAR LABELED "THE EXACT PHRASE" FUNCTIONS AS QUOTATION MARKS, ISOLATING THAT PRECISE STRING OF WORDS WITHIN A WEBSITE. "ANY OF THESE WORDS" WORKS LIKE AN "OR" SEARCH. AND "NONE OF THESE WORDS" IS A "**NOT**" SEARCH.

BOOLEAN
- AND
- OR
- NOT

GOOGLE ADVANCED
- ALL THESE WORDS
- ANY of THESE WORDS
- NONE of THESE WORDS

GOOGLE SHORTCUT
- JUST TYPE IN YOUR TERMS— GOOGLE AUTOMATICALLY TREATS IT AS AN **AND** SEARCH
- TYPE IN **OR** BETWEEN YOUR TERMS
- PUT A **MINUS** SIGN NEXT TO WORDS YOU DON'T WANT

IN MANY WAYS, THIS IS EASIER THAN A CATALOG OR DATABASE SEARCH. IT'S MORE OBVIOUS EXACTLY HOW TERMS ARE USED TO NARROW OR EXPAND SEARCHES, AND IT ELIMINATES THE NEED TO USE A COMBINATION OF SEARCH TERMS, BOOLEAN OPERATORS, AND PARENTHESES. JUST PLUG YOUR SEARCH TERMS INTO THE APPROPRIATE BOXES AND GO!*

*TRY USING GOOGLE'S OWN TIPS AT http://www.powersearchingwithgoogle.com/.

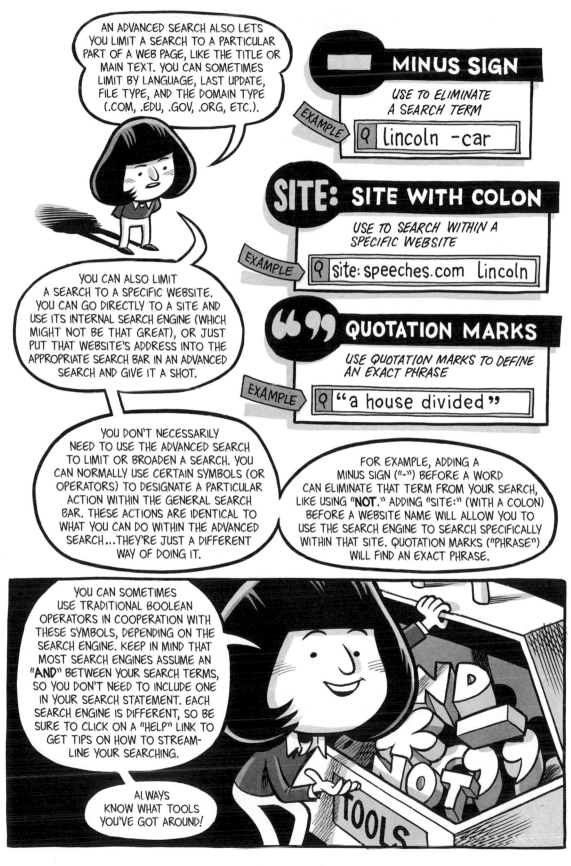

AN ADVANCED SEARCH ALSO LETS YOU LIMIT A SEARCH TO A PARTICULAR PART OF A WEB PAGE, LIKE THE TITLE OR MAIN TEXT. YOU CAN SOMETIMES LIMIT BY LANGUAGE, LAST UPDATE, FILE TYPE, AND THE DOMAIN TYPE (.COM, .EDU, .GOV, .ORG, ETC.).

MINUS SIGN

USE TO ELIMINATE A SEARCH TERM

EXAMPLE

Q lincoln -car

YOU CAN ALSO LIMIT A SEARCH TO A SPECIFIC WEBSITE. YOU CAN GO DIRECTLY TO A SITE AND USE ITS INTERNAL SEARCH ENGINE (WHICH MIGHT NOT BE THAT GREAT), OR JUST PUT THAT WEBSITE'S ADDRESS INTO THE APPROPRIATE SEARCH BAR IN AN ADVANCED SEARCH AND GIVE IT A SHOT.

SITE: **SITE WITH COLON**

USE TO SEARCH WITHIN A SPECIFIC WEBSITE

EXAMPLE

Q site: speeches.com lincoln

" " QUOTATION MARKS

USE QUOTATION MARKS TO DEFINE AN EXACT PHRASE

EXAMPLE

Q "a house divided"

YOU DON'T NECESSARILY NEED TO USE THE ADVANCED SEARCH TO LIMIT OR BROADEN A SEARCH. YOU CAN NORMALLY USE CERTAIN SYMBOLS (OR OPERATORS) TO DESIGNATE A PARTICULAR ACTION WITHIN THE GENERAL SEARCH BAR. THESE ACTIONS ARE IDENTICAL TO WHAT YOU CAN DO WITHIN THE ADVANCED SEARCH...THEY'RE JUST A DIFFERENT WAY OF DOING IT.

FOR EXAMPLE, ADDING A MINUS SIGN ("-") BEFORE A WORD CAN ELIMINATE THAT TERM FROM YOUR SEARCH, LIKE USING "**NOT**." ADDING "**SITE:**" (WITH A COLON) BEFORE A WEBSITE NAME WILL ALLOW YOU TO USE THE SEARCH ENGINE TO SEARCH SPECIFICALLY WITHIN THAT SITE. QUOTATION MARKS ("PHRASE") WILL FIND AN EXACT PHRASE.

YOU CAN SOMETIMES USE TRADITIONAL BOOLEAN OPERATORS IN COOPERATION WITH THESE SYMBOLS, DEPENDING ON THE SEARCH ENGINE. KEEP IN MIND THAT MOST SEARCH ENGINES ASSUME AN "**AND**" BETWEEN YOUR SEARCH TERMS, SO YOU DON'T NEED TO INCLUDE ONE IN YOUR SEARCH STATEMENT. EACH SEARCH ENGINE IS DIFFERENT, SO BE SURE TO CLICK ON A "HELP" LINK TO GET TIPS ON HOW TO STREAM-LINE YOUR SEARCHING.

ALWAYS KNOW WHAT TOOLS YOU'VE GOT AROUND!

TOOLS

ALL WEBSITES ABOUT INFORMATION LITERACY

.edu .com .mil .info .net .gov .org

SEARCH ENGINES AREN'T THE ONLY GATEWAYS TO INFORMATION ON THE OPEN WEB. DEPENDING ON YOUR RESEARCH, IT MIGHT BE A GOOD IDEA TO CHECK OUT VARIOUS GOVERNMENT, PUBLIC, AND NONPROFIT ORGANIZATIONS' WEBSITES. THEY USUALLY HAVE FREELY AVAILABLE INFORMATIONAL OR RESEARCH-BASED DIGITAL RESOURCES.

REMEMBER THAT YOU CAN SEARCH A SPECIFIC DOMAIN, LIKE .GOV, WITHIN A GOOGLE ADVANCED SEARCH. THIS COULD BE HANDY IF YOU WANTED RESULTS ON A TOPIC ONLY FROM ONE TYPE OF SITE. FOR EXAMPLE, LET'S SAY I WANTED TO FIND MATERIAL ON PUBLIC INFORMATION LITERACY POLICY AND INITIATIVES. I COULD DO A GOOGLE SEARCH FOR "INFORMATION LITERACY" AND LIMIT THE SEARCH TO .GOV SITES, AND I WOULD GET RESULTS ON THAT TOPIC FROM FEDERAL, STATE, AND SOME LOCAL GOVERNMENT SITES.

THERE'S AN OVERWHELMING VOLUME OF OFFICIAL INFORMATION PUBLISHED BY THE GOVERNMENT, AN INCREASING AMOUNT OF WHICH CAN BE FOUND ONLINE.

THE U.S. GOVERNMENT PRINTING OFFICE (GPO) KEEPS A GREAT COLLECTION OF DIGITAL RESOURCES DETAILING THE INNER WORKINGS AND PROCESSES OF OUR GOVERNMENT AT www.gpo.gov.

THE LIBRARY OF CONGRESS PROVIDES ACCESS TO MANY DIGITAL RESOURCES RELATED TO THE HISTORY OF THE UNITED STATES, AND IT OFFERS LINKS TO VARIOUS GOVERNMENTAL DEPARTMENTS, OFFICES, AND FOUNDATIONS, MANY OF WHICH OFFER THEIR OWN PUBLICATIONS AND RESEARCH. FIND IT ALL AT www.loc.gov.

www.science.gov COMPILES AND LETS YOU SEARCH THROUGH VAST AMOUNTS OF SCIENTIFIC RESEARCH FROM MULTIPLE GOVERNMENT AGENCIES WITH ONE SEARCH, AND www.congress.gov SUPPLIES AN ENORMOUS AMOUNT OF LEGISLATIVE INFORMATION.

THE FEDERAL GOVERNMENT ALSO DEDICATES BILLIONS OF DOLLARS EACH YEAR TOWARD FUNDING OUTSIDE RESEARCH. THERE'S BEEN A REAL PUSH FOR INCREASED TRANSPARENCY IN THAT RESEARCH, SO WE CAN EXPECT MORE ACCESS TO FEDERALLY FUNDED RESEARCH VERY SOON, FINGERS CROSSED.

IF YOU DON'T HAVE INTERNET ACCESS, OR JUST CAN'T FIND THE RESOURCES YOU'RE LOOKING FOR, CHECK TO SEE IF YOUR LOCAL LIBRARY HAS BEEN DESIGNATED A **FEDERAL DEPOSITORY**. IF SO, THEY'LL HAVE GOVERNMENT PUBLICATIONS YOU CAN ACCESS IN PRINT AND ONLINE.

THIS LOOKS LIKE A GOOD SPOT TO KEEP THIS STUFF!

LIBRARY

IN ADDITION TO RESEARCH AND INFORMATION MADE AVAILABLE BY THE GOVERNMENT AND OTHER PUBLICLY ORIENTED ORGANIZATIONS, LIBRARIES, ARCHIVES, AND MUSEUMS ALMOST ALWAYS HAVE EXHIBITIONS AND SPECIAL COLLECTIONS THAT ARE SEARCHABLE ONLINE AND INCREASINGLY AVAILABLE IN THEIR ENTIRETY AS DIGITAL COLLECTIONS. FOR AN EXAMPLE, SEE THE SMITHSONIAN INSTITUTE ONLINE AT www.si.edu.

GOT ONE MORE THING TO LOAD UP FOR YA.

I DON'T THINK IT'LL FIT...

APOLLO 11 ARTIFACTS

WHAT IF YOU DON'T KNOW WHICH ORGANIZATIONS ARE DOING RESEARCH ON YOUR TOPIC? WELL, IF YOU'VE ALREADY FOUND SOME USEFUL ARTICLES, BOOKS, OR WEBSITES, TAKE A CLOSER LOOK AT THE AUTHORS TO SEE IF YOU CAN DETERMINE WHERE THEY WORK AND WHERE THE RESEARCH IS BEING PERFORMED.

YOU'VE PROBABLY ALREADY DONE A GOOGLE SEARCH FOR YOUR TOPIC. TRY AGAIN AND THIS TIME TAKE A CLOSE LOOK AT WHO IS PRODUCING THE INFORMATION. YOU MIGHT ALSO ADD "RESEARCH" TO YOUR SEARCH TERMS TO EMPHASIZE THAT FOCUS. YOU COULD LIMIT THE SEARCH TO .EDU, .GOV, OR MAYBE .ORG DOMAINS.

BE FLEXIBLE AND DIRECT WITH YOUR SEARCHES. DON'T BE AFRAID TO PLUG IN VARIANTS FOR YOUR TERMS IF YOUR SEARCH ISN'T WORKING. YOU MIGHT FIND WHOLE "TEAMS" OF RESEARCHERS DEVOTED TO INVESTIGATING DIFFERENT ASPECTS OF YOUR TOPIC!

WE'RE GONNA BEAT THE PEER REVIEW OUTTA YOU!!

DISSERTATION DEFENSE!

DATA

RUTHERFORD STATE RESEARCHERS

ALL RIGHT, FOLKS. IT'S DOWN TO THE WIRE. YOU GET OUT THERE AND DO WHAT YOU DO. RESEARCH! RESEARCH WITH EVERYTHING YOU'VE GOT!

OF COURSE, YOU WILL NEED TO EVALUATE EACH RESOURCE TO DETERMINE WHETHER OR NOT YOU CAN TRUST THE INFORMATION. WE'LL GET INTO THAT MORE LATER, BUT HERE'S A QUICK EXAMPLE:

I DID A SIMPLE GOOGLE SEARCH FOR "ASTEROID RESEARCH" AND FOUND LEGITIMATE RESEARCH DONE BY THE ASTEROID DEFLECTION RESEARCH CENTER (YES, A REAL PLACE) DEDICATED TO COMING UP WITH WAYS TO KNOCK THREATENING ASTEROIDS OFF COURSE. I ALSO FOUND A WEBSITE THAT PRESENTED AN EMOTIONAL APPEAL TO READERS ABOUT THE INEVITABILITY OF A LARGE ASTEROID STRIKING EARTH IN THE HOPE OF RAISING FUNDS FOR RESEARCH EQUIPMENT.

RELEVANT RESEARCH CONTENT

THAT WAS A FAIRLY VAGUE SEARCH IN THE FIRST PLACE, BUT IT ILLUSTRATES THE FACT THAT YOU WILL FIND MANY SITES DEDICATED TO A TOPIC AND YOU WILL NEED TO EVALUATE THEM IN ORDER TO TARGET RELEVANT CONTENT.

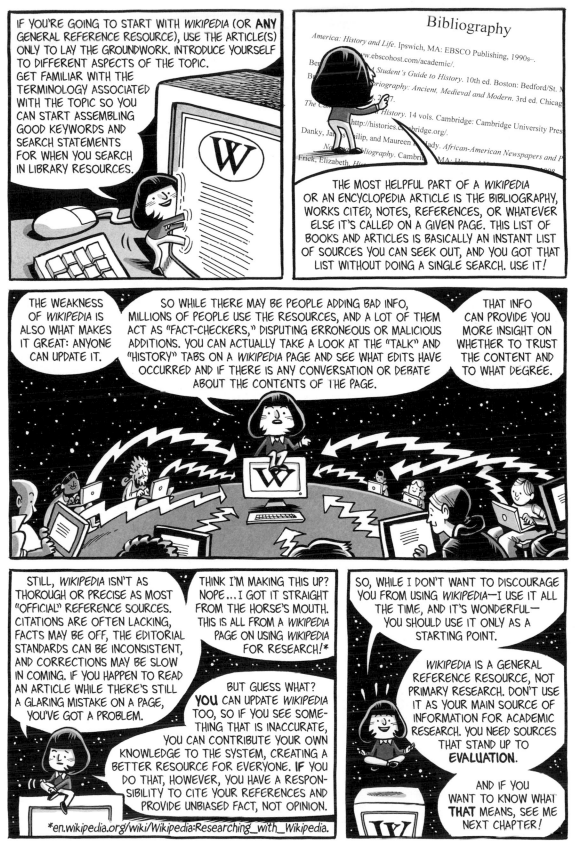

CRITICAL THINKING EXERCISES

1. Do a Google search for your topic using the search statement(s) you've developed. How many results do you get? How many results on the **first** page seem to be relevant to your topic? How about on the second through tenth pages? Be sure to examine the sites for clues to the purpose and context of the content.

2. How could you use what you know about search strategies to help narrow (or broaden) your Google results and ensure that you get a higher percentage of relevant and useful results earlier in your list?

3. Attempt to identify a website for an organization that provides information on your topic. This might be a public, government, or educational organization. Be sure to browse the site for information about the organization, including their purpose and resources. For example, if I am interested in the history of spaceflight, I might take a look at the National Air and Space Museum's website, collections, mission, and online resources. What site(s) can you identify, and why might they be helpful or harmful to your research?

4. Investigate and describe how to edit a *Wikipedia* page. Explain how information on *Wikipedia* is verified and accepted or not accepted. How do these guidelines, policies, and procedures alter your understanding of *Wikipedia* and how you use the information on the website?

5. Find a *Wikipedia* article (or articles) relevant to your topic. Explain how these articles can be useful to your research and how they should be used within the context of an academic assignment.

6. How could you use a *Wikipedia* article to expand your research and find more information on the topic within your own library's resources?

CHAPTER SIX
EVALUATING YOUR SOURCES

BOOK

WE'VE ALLUDED TO THAT A NUMBER OF TIMES, BUT WE HAVEN'T REALLY TALKED ABOUT HOW TO DETERMINE IF A SOURCE IS WORTH USING IN YOUR RESEARCH. THERE ARE GOOD SOURCES, BAD SOURCES, AND IN-BETWEEN SOURCES. AND THE QUALITY OF THOSE SOURCES CAN SHIFT DEPENDING ON THE CONTEXT OF YOUR OWN NEEDS.

NOT ALL INFORMATION IS EQUAL.

SO LET'S TALK ABOUT HOW TO EFFECTIVELY EXAMINE A SOURCE AND JUDGE THE QUALITY OF ITS INFORMATION.

FEMA ATF

THIS PROCESS CAN BE RELATIVE: DEPENDING ON YOUR RESEARCH TOPIC AND THE APPROACH YOU'RE TAKING, A SOURCE CAN BE EITHER GOOD **OR** BAD; **MORE** USEFUL OR **LESS** USEFUL.

FOR EXAMPLE, IF I'M STUDYING THE LOCAL, STATE, AND FEDERAL AUTHORITIES' RESPONSES TO A NATURAL DISASTER, THE GENERAL PUBLIC'S TWITTER RESPONSES WON'T NECESSARILY PROVIDE THE INFORMATION I NEED. I COULD LOOK AT THE RELEVANT GOVERNMENT WEBSITES AND MAYBE EVEN **THEIR** TWITTER FEEDS FOR QUALITY INFORMATION, BUT I'D HAVE TO BE SPECIFIC.

IF, HOWEVER, I WANT TO RESEARCH HOW INFORMATION (OR MISINFORMATION) IS SPREAD VIA TWITTER DURING THAT DISASTER, I WOULD DEFINITELY WANT TO INCLUDE THE TWEETS OF THE GENERAL PUBLIC IN MY STUDY.

IN THE FIRST CASE, THE INFORMATION FOUND IN THOSE CIVILIAN TWEETS MAY NOT BE RELEVANT OR ACCURATE, BUT A CHANGE IN PERSPECTIVE SUDDENLY MADE THEM RELEVANT AND USEFUL. SO AS YOU CAN SEE, YOUR POINT OF VIEW AND RESEARCH ANGLE HAS A BIG IMPACT ON WHAT KIND OF INFORMATION YOU NEED.

EXAMINE EACH SOURCE YOU USE, WHETHER IT'S FROM AN ACADEMIC JOURNAL, POPULAR MAGAZINE, BOOK, WEBSITE, OR A PERSON YELLING ON THE STREET CORNER. EVERY PIECE OF INFORMATION NEEDS TO BE EVALUATED; THERE ARE MULTIPLE FACTORS CONTRIBUTING TO A SOURCE'S USEFULNESS.

JUST BECAUSE A SOURCE IS "ACADEMIC" DOESN'T MEAN IT'S RIGHT FOR YOUR RESEARCH. EVEN QUALITY SOURCES CAN BE IRRELEVANT TO YOUR WORK.

ON THE FLIP SIDE, JUST BECAUSE SOMETHING IS "POPULAR" DOESN'T NECESSARILY ELIMINATE IT FROM YOUR LIST OF RESOURCES, ESPECIALLY IF THE APPROACH YOU'RE TAKING REQUIRES A POPULAR VIEWPOINT.

EVALUATION IS AN ONGOING PROCESS. DON'T COMPILE A TON OF RESOURCES AND EVALUATE THEM ALL AT THE SAME TIME. LOCATE A RESOURCE, EVALUATE IT, AND DECIDE WHETHER OR NOT TO KEEP IT BEFORE MOVING ON TO THE NEXT.

THIS LETS YOU BUILD A CORE SET OF SOURCES LIKELY TO HAVE IMMEDIATE IMPACT ON YOUR RESEARCH, INSTEAD OF A BIG MESS YOU HAVE TO SORT THROUGH LATER.

EVALUATING INFORMATION ISN'T IMPORTANT JUST FOR SCHOOL RESEARCH.

QUALITY INFORMATION CAN HELP YOU DECIDE WHAT CAR TO PURCHASE OR WHICH DOCTOR TO SEE. BEING A CRITICAL USER OF INFORMATION CAN HELP YOU BE MORE USEFUL AND PRODUCTIVE IN YOUR JOB, AS WELL. YOU MAY NEED TO RESEARCH THE COMPETITION OR FIGURE OUT HOW TO SOLVE A LEGAL QUESTION. KNOWING HOW TO TELL GOOD INFORMATION FROM BAD CAN BE A MAJOR FACTOR IN YOUR OVERALL SUCCESS.

BEING AN ACTIVE AND EFFECTIVE CITIZEN REQUIRES YOU TO BE INFORMED. THERE IS A LOT OF MISINFORMATION OUT THERE TO LEAD YOU ASTRAY. BEING ABLE TO EXAMINE THE QUALITY OF INFORMATION HELPS YOU BECOME MORE ABLE TO ACT—AND VOTE—IN AN EDUCATED, RESPONSIBLE MANNER.

CHAPTER SIX

*SEE L. TOWNSEND, K. BRUNETTI, AND A. R. HOFER, "THRESHOLD CONCEPTS AND INFORMATION LITERACY," PORTAL: LIBRARIES AND THE ACADEMY 11, NO. 3 (2011): 853–69; AND THE ACRL DRAFT FRAMEWORK FOR INFORMATION LITERACY FOR HIGHER EDUCATION, AT acrl.ala.org/ilstandards/wp-content/uploads/2014/04/Framework-for-IL-for-HE-Draft-1-Part-2.pdf.

YOU'LL ALSO WANT TO ASK, "WHO IS THE INFORMATION FOR? WHO IS THE AUDIENCE?"

IT'S COMING RIGHT AT US!

Doomsday Rock to Collide with EARTH?

How to Spot Near-Earth Objects from your Backyard

Compositional Analysis and Distribution of S-Type Near-Earth Objects

KNOWING A SOURCE'S TARGET AUDIENCE HELPS DETERMINE WHETHER OR NOT THE SOURCE WILL BE APPROPRIATE FOR YOUR RESEARCH. OBVIOUSLY, AN ARTICLE FROM THE *JOURNAL OF ASTROPHYSICS* IS GOING TO HAVE A PARTICULAR AUDIENCE IN MIND, SO PAY ATTENTION TO THE TITLES OF THE PUBLICATION OR WEBSITE.

ACADEMIC SOURCES ARE AIMED AT AUDIENCES KNOWLEDGEABLE ABOUT SPECIFIC TOPICS, AND POPULAR SOURCES ARE AIMED AT AN AUDIENCE THAT MAY HAVE NO SUCH PRIOR KNOWLEDGE. FOR ACADEMIC RESEARCH, YOU PROBABLY WANT TO USE AN ACADEMIC SOURCE, BUT EVEN THOSE CAN HAVE VARYING AUDIENCES IN MIND.

LOOK AT THE LANGUAGE IN THE SOURCE. IS IT TOO TECHNICAL AND JARGON-FILLED FOR YOU TO UNDERSTAND AND USE EFFECTIVELY? OR IS IT TOO SIMPLE, OFFERING ONLY A BASIC EXPLANATION OF A TOPIC THAT ISN'T ADVANCED ENOUGH FOR YOUR NEEDS?

TOO SIMPLE OR GENERAL

JUST RIGHT

TOO ADVANCED AND COMPLICATE[D]

HEY!

YOU SHOULD ALSO LOOK AT THE **SCOPE** OF THE SOURCE. DOES IT COVER BROAD ASPECTS OF A TOPIC OR VERY DETAILED SPECIFICS? AGAIN, WHAT ARE YOUR RESEARCH NEEDS?

DOES THE SOURCE REPEAT INFORMATION YOU ALREADY KNOW, OR DOES IT PROVIDE NEW INSIGHT OR INFORMATION OF WHICH YOU WERE PREVIOUSLY UNAWARE?

THIS CAN BE A VERY RELATIVE PROCESS, SO IT'S IMPORTANT THAT YOU DETERMINE YOUR NEEDS EARLY ON. ARE YOU WRITING A BASIC OVERVIEW OF THE TOPIC? ARE YOU CREATING A LESSON FOR CHILDREN, OR PRESENTING TO YOUR PEERS IN A GRAD-UATE COURSE? ARE YOU WRITING AN ADVANCED RESEARCH PAPER?

Advanced Quark Theory

HEY! ...

...YOU SAVAGES AREN'T EVEN LISTENING!

YOUR AUDIENCE SHIFTS THE FOCUS YOU'RE LOOKING FOR IN YOUR SOURCES.

NOW, EVEN MORE QUESTIONS: WHY WAS THIS INFORMATION CREATED? HOW DOES THE AUTHOR HOPE TO **IMPACT** THE AUDIENCE? WHAT'S THE PURPOSE? YOU NEED TO KNOW THIS SO YOU CAN UNDERSTAND HOW THE AUTHOR IS APPROACHING THE TOPIC. THE PURPOSE OF A SOURCE CAN CHANGE HOW WE VIEW AND USE IT.

AUDIENCE

AUTHOR

http://www.marsden4mayor.com

MARSDEN 4 MAYOR

Let me explain why I'm right and my opponent is wrong without really answering your question or addressing the issue.

Click here for FREE BUMPER STICKER!

SOMETIMES, INFORMATION IS MEANT TO PERSUADE OR CONVINCE THE AUDIENCE OF SOMETHING. THIS APPROACH IS NOT **GUARANTEED** TO BE UNTRUST-WORTHY, BUT BE CAREFUL WHEN AN AUTHOR CLEARLY TAKES A SIDE ON A TOPIC. MAKE SURE THAT ANY OPPOSING VIEWPOINTS ARE ACKNOWLEDGED AND SATISFACTORILY ADDRESSED BEFORE YOU CONSIDER USING A PERSUASIVE SOURCE IN YOUR RESEARCH.

SOMETIMES INFORMATION IS INTENDED TO SELL THE AUDIENCE SOMETHING. SOMETIMES IT'S OBVIOUS, BUT OFTEN THE AUTHORS ATTEMPT TO HIDE THEIR INTENTIONS OR PROVIDE MISLEADING, EVEN FALSE STATISTICS TO HELP SEAL THE DEAL.

According to recent research, owning an Icarus Sunflare increases your attractiveness by 46%, your job success by 19%, and your debt by 174%.*

*Results provided by Daedalus Innovations, a parent company of Icarus Automobiles, but don't worry, just go with it.

INFORMATION DESIGNED FOR ENTERTAINMENT OR SATIRE IS OFTEN FULL OF FALSE STATEMENTS AND IMAGINARY "FACTS," BUT IT IS SOMETIMES DISGUISED AS ACTUAL NEWS OR SCHOLARLY INFORMATION. DON'T MISTAKE SATIRE FOR REALITY!

THE NOT NRN REAL NEWS

Congress Begins Third Hibernation of the Year: Senator Marcus (D-OR) Gains 45 Pounds to "Keep Me Satisfied Until the Next Session."

AND, OF COURSE, INFORMATION CAN BE USED TO... **INFORM**. OBJECTIVE, UNBIASED, FACTUAL INFORMATION USED TO EDUCATE. YEP, IT CAN BE THAT SIMPLE.*

YOU'LL NORMALLY FOCUS ON THIS TYPE OF INFORMATION FOR RESEARCH PROJECTS, BUT REMEMBER THIS CAN DEPEND ON WHAT YOU'RE RESEARCHING AND HOW YOU CHOOSE TO APPROACH THE TOPIC.

the JOURNAL of STRAIGHTFORWARD INFORMATION

*HOWEVER, YOU CAN ALMOST ALWAYS FIND SOMETHING TO COMPLAIN ABOUT WITH **ANY** SOURCE, SO REMEMBER THAT OBJECTIVITY IS SOMETIMES JUST A BEST EFFORT.

CHAPTER SIX

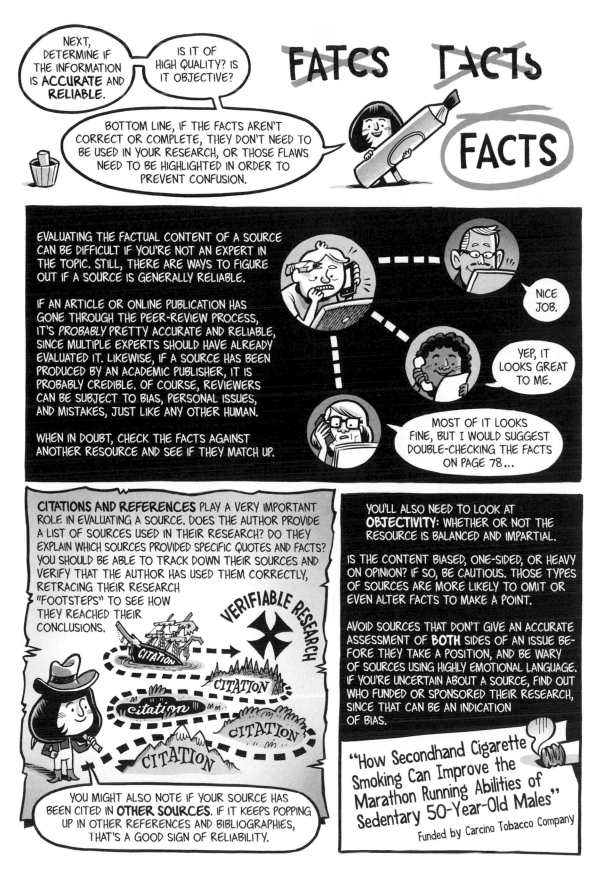

NEXT, DETERMINE IF THE INFORMATION IS **ACCURATE** AND **RELIABLE**.

IS IT OF HIGH QUALITY? IS IT OBJECTIVE?

BOTTOM LINE, IF THE FACTS AREN'T CORRECT OR COMPLETE, THEY DON'T NEED TO BE USED IN YOUR RESEARCH, OR THOSE FLAWS NEED TO BE HIGHLIGHTED IN ORDER TO PREVENT CONFUSION.

FATCS ~~FACTS~~ FACTS

EVALUATING THE FACTUAL CONTENT OF A SOURCE CAN BE DIFFICULT IF YOU'RE NOT AN EXPERT IN THE TOPIC. STILL, THERE ARE WAYS TO FIGURE OUT IF A SOURCE IS GENERALLY RELIABLE.

IF AN ARTICLE OR ONLINE PUBLICATION HAS GONE THROUGH THE PEER-REVIEW PROCESS, IT'S PROBABLY PRETTY ACCURATE AND RELIABLE, SINCE MULTIPLE EXPERTS SHOULD HAVE ALREADY EVALUATED IT. LIKEWISE, IF A SOURCE HAS BEEN PRODUCED BY AN ACADEMIC PUBLISHER, IT IS PROBABLY CREDIBLE. OF COURSE, REVIEWERS CAN BE SUBJECT TO BIAS, PERSONAL ISSUES, AND MISTAKES, JUST LIKE ANY OTHER HUMAN.

WHEN IN DOUBT, CHECK THE FACTS AGAINST ANOTHER RESOURCE AND SEE IF THEY MATCH UP.

NICE JOB.

YEP, IT LOOKS GREAT TO ME.

MOST OF IT LOOKS FINE, BUT I WOULD SUGGEST DOUBLE-CHECKING THE FACTS ON PAGE 78...

CITATIONS AND REFERENCES PLAY A VERY IMPORTANT ROLE IN EVALUATING A SOURCE. DOES THE AUTHOR PROVIDE A LIST OF SOURCES USED IN THEIR RESEARCH? DO THEY EXPLAIN WHICH SOURCES PROVIDED SPECIFIC QUOTES AND FACTS? YOU SHOULD BE ABLE TO TRACK DOWN THEIR SOURCES AND VERIFY THAT THE AUTHOR HAS USED THEM CORRECTLY, RETRACING THEIR RESEARCH "FOOTSTEPS" TO SEE HOW THEY REACHED THEIR CONCLUSIONS.

VERIFIABLE RESEARCH

CITATION
CITATION
citation
CITATION
CITATION

YOU MIGHT ALSO NOTE IF YOUR SOURCE HAS BEEN CITED IN **OTHER SOURCES**. IF IT KEEPS POPPING UP IN OTHER REFERENCES AND BIBLIOGRAPHIES, THAT'S A GOOD SIGN OF RELIABILITY.

YOU'LL ALSO NEED TO LOOK AT **OBJECTIVITY**: WHETHER OR NOT THE RESOURCE IS BALANCED AND IMPARTIAL.

IS THE CONTENT BIASED, ONE-SIDED, OR HEAVY ON OPINION? IF SO, BE CAUTIOUS. THOSE TYPES OF SOURCES ARE MORE LIKELY TO OMIT OR EVEN ALTER FACTS TO MAKE A POINT.

AVOID SOURCES THAT DON'T GIVE AN ACCURATE ASSESSMENT OF **BOTH** SIDES OF AN ISSUE BEFORE THEY TAKE A POSITION, AND BE WARY OF SOURCES USING HIGHLY EMOTIONAL LANGUAGE. IF YOU'RE UNCERTAIN ABOUT A SOURCE, FIND OUT WHO FUNDED OR SPONSORED THEIR RESEARCH, SINCE THAT CAN BE AN INDICATION OF BIAS.

"How Secondhand Cigarette Smoking Can Improve the Marathon Running Abilities of Sedentary 50-Year-Old Males"

Funded by Carcino Tobacco Company

PROBABLY THE MOST FUNDAMENTAL QUESTION YOU SHOULD ASK ABOUT A SOURCE IS, DOES IT CONTRIBUTE TO YOUR WORK? IS IT SOMETHING YOU CAN USE FOR YOUR RESEARCH, OR IS IT BETTER LEFT OUT?

HOW **RELEVANT** IS THE SOURCE TO YOUR RESEARCH? OBVIOUSLY, A BOOK ON ABRAHAM LINCOLN WON'T BE RELEVANT TO A RESEARCH PROJECT ON THE PHYSICS OF BASEBALL.

WELL, **PROBABLY** NOT, ANYWAY.

FOUR RUNS AND SEVEN INNINGS AGO...

SOMETIMES IT'S MORE COMPLICATED AND NUANCED THAN THAT. A MORE PRECISE QUESTION MIGHT BE, HOW DIRECTLY DOES THE SOURCE ADDRESS YOUR OWN RESEARCH?

ANOTHER WAY TO GAUGE RELEVANCE IS TO EXAMINE HOW MUCH OVERLAP A SOURCE SHARES WITH YOUR TOPIC. ABE LINCOLN AND BASEBALL PHYSICS HAVE ZERO OVERLAP, BUT AN ARTICLE ON FREQUENT EXERCISE FOR OLDER PERSONS MIGHT BE AN EXCELLENT FIT FOR, SAY, RESEARCHING WHAT FACTORS HELP PEOPLE LIVE LONGER.

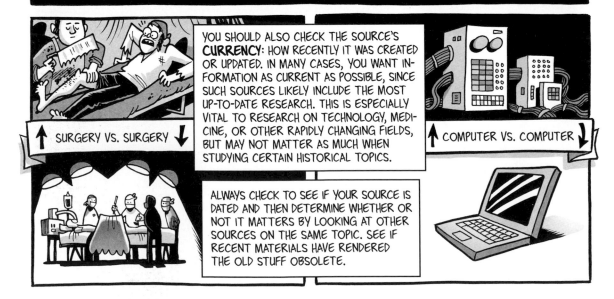

YOU SHOULD ALSO CHECK THE SOURCE'S **CURRENCY**: HOW RECENTLY IT WAS CREATED OR UPDATED. IN MANY CASES, YOU WANT IN-FORMATION AS CURRENT AS POSSIBLE, SINCE SUCH SOURCES LIKELY INCLUDE THE MOST UP-TO-DATE RESEARCH. THIS IS ESPECIALLY VITAL TO RESEARCH ON TECHNOLOGY, MEDI-CINE, OR OTHER RAPIDLY CHANGING FIELDS, BUT MAY NOT MATTER AS MUCH WHEN STUDYING CERTAIN HISTORICAL TOPICS.

SURGERY VS. SURGERY

COMPUTER VS. COMPUTER

ALWAYS CHECK TO SEE IF YOUR SOURCE IS DATED AND THEN DETERMINE WHETHER OR NOT IT MATTERS BY LOOKING AT OTHER SOURCES ON THE SAME TOPIC. SEE IF RECENT MATERIALS HAVE RENDERED THE OLD STUFF OBSOLETE.

CHAPTER SIX

CRITICAL THINKING EXERCISES

1. Locate at least one book, one scholarly article, and one web resource relevant to your topic. Evaluate each resource by examining the author/creator, intended audience, purpose, accuracy, currency, objectivity, and relevance. How does the process of evaluating sources help you determine whether or not to use a source in your research?

2. What kind of "information bias" do you have? Are you more likely to access, consume, and believe content made available through certain media? Do your preferences change depending on your information need? How so? Is there a particular author, website, show, or other media that you are unwilling or uncomfortable dealing with? Identify some types of information you knowingly avoid and attempt to assess why you feel a certain way about that info. Take time to evaluate the source(s) and try to imagine possible scenarios in which that particular information would be relevant to someone. Do you feel that your preferences are justified, or have you discovered new potential sources of useful information?

3. How do you feel about using information that you find through Facebook, Twitter, and other social media in your own research? Remember that even though you might initially locate information through social media, you could actually be sent to another site through a link to actually access the content. How could you determine the authority of an author who posts something online through social media?

4. Find a resource on your topic that you would not use in your research. Explain why you would avoid it, using the criteria noted above.

5. Find an academic journal article on your topic, as well as one from a popular magazine, newspaper, or website. Compare the two. How do they differ in terms of language, length, content, citation, and authority? How do these differences affect the potential use of the articles?

6. Is your research topic dependent on the most up-to-date information and research? Why or why not?

7. Examine a satirical news site like the *Onion*, the *Daily Currant*, or the *Duffel Blog*. What is the purpose of websites like these? Would you use these sites for a research project? Why or why not? What clues help you determine if the information is accurate or not?

USING INFORMATION ETHICALLY

PLAGIARISM
CITATION

A LOT OF STUDENTS HEAR THE TERMS **PLAGIARISM** AND **CITATION** AND IMMEDIATELY COLLAPSE IN GIBBERING, INCOHERENT TERROR. YOU DON'T NEED TO BE SCARED. THE SUBJECT'S A **LOT** LESS COMPLICATED THAN YOU THINK.

FIRST OF ALL, LET'S DEFINE THE TERMS.

PLAGIARISM

IS THE ACT OF TAKING SOMEONE ELSE'S WORK AND USING IT AS YOUR OWN, WITHOUT GIVING CREDIT TO THOSE WHO ACTUALLY DID THE RESEARCH AND WRITING.

RESEARCH

IT'S INTELLECTUAL THIEVERY. SIMPLY PUT, IT'S STEALING.

SO, HOW DO YOU REFER TO SOMEONE ELSE'S WORK WITHOUT PLAGIARIZING IT? WHAT TORTUOUS AND CONVOLUTED PROCESS MUST YOU GO THROUGH TO ENSURE THAT YOUR WORK IS YOUR OWN AND THAT YOU'RE NOT ACCUSED OF STEALING?

IT'S ACTUALLY VERY, VERY SIMPLE: **GIVE CREDIT WHERE CREDIT IS DUE.**

THIS IS CALLED **CITATION.**

REMEMBER, RESEARCH IS A COLLECTIVE PROCESS, ONE SHARED AND ADDED TO BY ALL RESEARCHERS. AS A RESEARCHER, YOU CONTRIBUTE TO THE PROCESS BY BUILDING ON THE WORK OF OTHERS. YOU'RE NOT DOING ANYTHING WRONG BY USING THE RESEARCH OTHERS HAVE ALREADY DONE. THAT'S OK. THAT'S THE **POINT!** THE BODY OF RESEARCH GROWS THROUGH THE YEARS BECAUSE PEOPLE REACH NEW CONCLUSIONS AND MAKE NEW DISCOVERIES, EACH ONE BUILT OFF OF ITS PREDECESSORS IN SOME WAY.

USING THE WORK OF OTHERS IS OK. IN FACT, YOU KIND OF HAVE TO... OTHERWISE YOU START FROM SCRATCH.

YOU JUST HAVE TO REMEMBER TO **GIVE CREDIT.**

NOW, IF YOU DIGEST AND CONDENSE AN IDEA, THAT'S CALLED **SUMMARIZING**. USING YOUR OWN WORDS TO EXPLAIN THE RESEARCH OF ANOTHER PERSON IN A FEW SENTENCES, WITHOUT DIRECTLY QUOTING OR PARAPHRASING THEM, IS SUMMARIZING.

YOU CAN TAKE MULTIPLE IDEAS FROM A SOURCE AND COMPRESS THEM INTO SOMETHING YOUR AUDIENCE CAN READ QUICKLY AND UNDERSTAND.

AUTHOR'S VERSION:

Almost instantly, the plane vanished from sight. Wind rushed past me as I plummeted to earth, my unopened parachute every bit as useless as those parcels of silverware and anvils that seem to plague parachutists in vintage cartoons. I envisioned an equally cartoonish end to my plunge, one that would result in my body punching a perfect me-shaped hole through the ground presently racing up to meet me. I laughed at the absurdity of the image even as my life flashed before my eyes...

SUMMARY:

Steve's parachute didn't open. He imagined himself as a cartoon character, complete with an anvil on his back and leaving a perfect Steve-shaped hole in the ground. The image made him laugh in spite of his impending demise.

NOW, NOT QUITE EVERYTHING NEEDS A CITATION. IF YOU HAVE FACTS IN YOUR PAPER THAT ARE COMMON KNOWLEDGE, NOT BASED ON SOMEONE ELSE'S WORDS OR ORIGINAL RESEARCH, THOSE FACTS DON'T REQUIRE CITATIONS.

FOR EXAMPLE, IF YOU SAY WORLD WAR II RESULTED IN THE DEATHS OF MILLIONS OF PEOPLE AROUND THE GLOBE, YOU DON'T NEED A CITATION. THAT'S COMMON KNOWLEDGE.

IF, HOWEVER, YOU WANT TO INCLUDE A SPECIFIC NUMBER OF DEATHS, YOU'LL NEED TO EXPLAIN WHERE YOU GOT THAT FIGURE, SINCE THERE ARE DIFFERENT ESTIMATES IN DIFFERENT SOURCES.

FLORIS

SALE

To my buddy, Steve. Sorry! Dude.

AS A RESEARCHER, YOU ARE (OR SHOULD BE) CREATING NEW KNOWLEDGE BY **SYNTHESIZING** THE VARIETY OF INFORMATION YOU'VE ENCOUNTERED INTO A NEW PRODUCT.

SURE, YOU'RE USING **EXISTING** RESEARCH AND INFORMATION, BUT YOU MAY BRING UNIQUE UNDERSTANDING AND EXPERIENCE TO THE TABLE THAT HELPS DEFINE THE NEW WORK AS YOUR OWN. YOUR AUDIENCE WILL STILL BE ABLE TO DISCERN THE MANY SOURCES (OR INGREDIENTS) YOU'VE USED...

...BUT THE FINAL PRODUCT SHOULD BE YOUR OWN CREATION, YOUR OWN UNDERSTANDING OF HOW ALL THE PIECES COME TOGETHER. YOU'RE NOT SIMPLY LISTING OR SUMMARIZING ALL THE OTHER RESEARCH OUT THERE. YOU'RE BUILDING A NEW UNDERSTANDING OF THAT RESEARCH AND CONTRIBUTING TO THE CONVERSATION!

CHAPTER SEVEN

CITATION LAND

PEER-REVIEWED PEAK

FULL CREDIT FOREST

Cross-Ref Creek

Monograph Marsh

RESEARCH ROAD

SO, YOU KNOW THAT TO AVOID PLAGIARISM, YOU EXPLAIN WHERE YOU GOT YOUR INFORMATION. BUT HOW DO YOU DO THAT? YOU DO THAT WITH **CITATION**, REMEMBER? CITATION IS JUST A WAY TO BRIEFLY DESCRIBE YOUR SOURCES SO READERS KNOW EXACTLY WHAT YOU USED IN YOUR RESEARCH AND WHERE THEY CAN FIND IT.

IT PROVIDES A ROAD MAP TO YOUR RESEARCH.

REMEMBER, RESEARCH IS A PROCESS THAT BUILDS CONTINUALLY UPON ITSELF. CITATIONS ARE AN EXAMPLE OF HOW NEW RESEARCH BUILDS ON OLDER RESEARCH. YOU CAN LOOK AT A BOOK OR ARTICLE AND TELL WHAT SOURCES THAT AUTHOR USED IN ORDER TO REACH THEIR OWN CONCLUSIONS. THINK OF RESEARCH AS AN ONGOING, NEVER-ENDING, ALWAYS-CHANGING **CONVERSATION.*** THERE ARE MANY VOICES AND VIEWPOINTS THAT CONTRIBUTE TO THE DISCUSSION, INCLUDING YOUR OWN! BE SURE TO ACT AS A RESPONSIBLE AND ETHICAL PARTICIPANT BY BEING HONEST WITH YOUR RESEARCH AND CITING THE WORK OF OTHERS.

WORKS CITED MIXER!

*SEE ACRL DRAFT OF FRAMEWORK FOR INFORMATION LITERACY FOR HIGHER EDUCATION, AT acrl.ala.org/ilstandards/wp-content/uploads/2014/02/ Framework-for-IL-for-HE-Draft-1-Part-1.pdf.

NOT ONLY DO CITATIONS KEEP YOU OUT OF TROUBLE—THE CITATIONS IN EACH OF YOUR SOURCES CAN ALSO HELP YOU FIND RESOURCES FOR YOUR OWN RESEARCH!

Bibliography

LET'S SAY YOU USE THE LIBRARY CATALOG OR DATABASE TO LOCATE A REALLY GOOD BOOK OR ARTICLE, BUT YOU DON'T FIND ANYTHING ELSE IN YOUR SEARCH RESULTS. WELL, **FLIP OR SCROLL TO THE END** OF THAT SOURCE.

THERE YOU'LL FIND THE LIST OF SOURCES THE AUTHOR USED, CALLED A BIBLIOGRAPHY, WORKS CITED, OR REFERENCES. THIS CAN BE A GOLD MINE! YOU MIGHT HAVE HUNDREDS OF POTENTIALLY USEFUL ITEMS LISTED FOR YOU RIGHT THERE! ALL YOU HAVE TO DO IS FIND THEM.

THEY MIGHT BE IN YOUR LIBRARY OR ITS DATABASES, OR YOU MIGHT HAVE TO REQUEST THEM FROM ANOTHER LIBRARY THROUGH INTERLIBRARY LOAN. THE POINT IS, SOMEONE HAS ALREADY DONE A TON OF RESEARCH ON YOUR TOPIC. BUILD ON WHAT THEY HAVE DONE, AND TRACK DOWN THE SOURCES THEY USED FOR THEIR RESEARCH.

WHO KNOWS, YOU MAY DISCOVER SOMETHING THAT THEY MISSED!

USING INFORMATION ETHICALLY

RESEARCH PAPERS CAN BE WRITTEN IN A VARIETY OF "STYLES." THERE ARE MULTIPLE STYLE MANUALS, EACH OFFERING DIFFERENT GUIDELINES FOR WRITING RESEARCH PAPERS.

MLA   APA   CHICAGO

SOME OF THE MOST COMMON GUIDES ARE THE MLA HANDBOOK FOR WRITERS OF RESEARCH PAPERS (MODERN LANGUAGE ASSOCIATION) STYLE MANUAL, THE PUBLICATION MANUAL OF THE AMERICAN PSYCHOLOGICAL ASSOCIATION (APA), AND THE CHICAGO MANUAL OF STYLE (OR A VARIATION KNOWN AS TURABIAN). THESE STYLES ARE TYPICALLY ASSOCIATED WITH DIFFERENT ACADEMIC DISCIPLINES. THOSE RESEARCH-ING IN THE HUMANITIES—AND ENGLISH, ESPECIALLY—WILL LIKELY USE MLA. THOSE IN THE SOCIAL SCIENCES ARE MORE LIKELY TO USE APA. HISTORY STUDENTS MOST OFTEN WRITE IN THE CHICAGO STYLE.*

THESE GUIDES PROVIDE INCREDIBLY DETAILED INSTRUCTIONS ON HOW TO WRITE AND FORMAT YOUR PAPER IN A PARTICULAR MANNER, BUT ONE AREA THAT RECEIVES A LOT OF ATTENTION IS HOW TO APPROPRIATELY CITE YOUR SOURCES OR REFERENCES. EACH CITATION STYLE LOOKS A LITTLE DIFFERENT, BUT THE PURPOSE IS THE SAME: EXPLAINING WHERE YOU GOT YOUR INFORMATION.

*NONE OF THAT IS SET IN STONE. YOU MAY FIND THAT YOUR INSTRUCTOR PREFERS A CERTAIN STYLE EVEN THOUGH IT'S NOT TYPICALLY USED IN THAT FIELD OF STUDY. AND THESE THREE AREN'T THE ONLY STYLES, BUT THEY ARE VERY TYPICAL FOR UNDERGRADUATE RESEARCH.

REGARDLESS OF STYLE, THERE ARE BASICALLY TWO MAJOR COMPONENTS WHEN IT COMES TO CITING SOURCES. ONE, A LITTLE NOTE NEXT TO EACH QUOTE, PARAPHRASE, OR SUMMARY, INDICATING WHICH SOURCE THAT INFORMATION CAME FROM, AND TWO, A LIST AT THE END OF YOUR PAPER SPECIFYING THE SOURCES YOU USED IN YOUR RESEARCH.

1. Tell us where it came from.

2. Tell us how to get to it.

THE FIRST COMPONENT TO CITING SOMETHING IS THE LITTLE NOTE EXPLAINING WHERE YOUR INFORMATION CAME FROM.

EACH TIME YOU USE INFORMATION FROM AN OUTSIDE SOURCE, YOU HAVE TO INDICATE TO YOUR READERS WHERE YOU OBTAINED THAT INFORMATION. IT'S NOT THE FULL REFERENCE...IT'S JUST A WAY TO CATCH THE READERS' ATTENTION AND MAKE SURE THEY KNOW THE INFORMATION IS FROM ANOTHER SOURCE.

DEPENDING ON THE STYLE YOU'RE USING, THIS CAN BE DONE IN A VARIETY OF WAYS.

IN-TEXT CITATIONS AND FOOTNOTES/ENDNOTES NOT ONLY TELL YOUR AUDIENCE THAT THE INFORMATION COMES FROM ANOTHER SOURCE; THEY ALSO DIRECT READERS TO THE COMPREHENSIVE LIST OF SOURCES YOU'LL INCLUDE AT THE END OF YOUR PAPER.

WORKS CITED
Thataway!

THAT LIST MUST INCLUDE ALL THE SOURCES YOU'VE USED IN YOUR RESEARCH. THIS LIST HAS A DIFFERENT NAME DEPENDING ON WHAT STYLE YOU'RE USING. APA TITLES IT "REFERENCES," MLA CALLS IT "WORKS CITED," WHILE CHICAGO STYLE OFTEN USES THE TERM "BIBLIOGRAPHY." WITHIN EACH LIST, NOTE EVERY SINGLE SOURCE YOU USED WHILE WRITING YOUR PAPER. THESE SOURCES ARE ORGANIZED ALPHABETICALLY BY THE AUTHOR'S LAST NAME. EACH STYLE PROVIDES A PARTICULAR STRUCTURE FOR ORGANIZING THE INFORMATION ABOUT YOUR SOURCE.

References

Works Cited

Bibliography

APA   MLA   CHICAGO

EACH STYLE PUTS CITATION DATA IN A DIFFERENT ORDER AND USES DIFFERENT INDICATORS (LIKE QUOTATION MARKS, ITALICS, AND OTHER PUNCTUATION) TO KEEP THE PARTS OF THE CITATION SEPARATE. AND EACH TYPE OF SOURCE (BOOK, ARTICLE, WEBSITE, ETC.) WILL BE CITED A BIT DIFFERENTLY, AS WELL, BECAUSE EACH TYPE CAN BE FOUND IN DIFFERENT WAYS. FOR EXAMPLE, ARTICLES WILL BE FOUND IN A SPECIFIC VOLUME AND ISSUE OF A PERIODICAL, BUT A BOOK STANDS ON ITS OWN.

STILL, REGARDLESS OF STYLE OR ITEM TYPE, YOU'LL NEED SIMILAR INFORMATION LIKE AUTHOR, TITLE, DATE, AND OTHER CLUES TO HELP READERS LOCATE THE UNIQUE RESOURCE.

PUBLISHER   MEDIUM
DOI   CHAPTER TITLE   PUBLISHER
WEB LOCATION   PLACE OF PUB.
PERIODICAL TITLE
EDITORS   BOOK TITLE
AUTHOR   CORPORATE AUTHOR
ARTICLE TITLE   DATE OF PUBLICATION

APA   MLA   CHICAGO
BOOK   PERIODICAL ARTICLE   WEB RESOURCE   OTHER

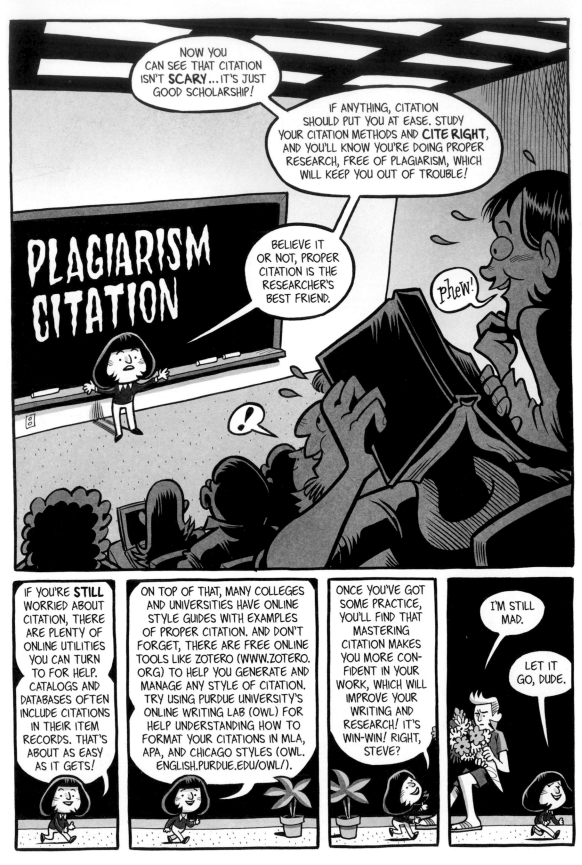

CHAPTER SEVEN

CHAPTER SEVEN

CHAPTER SEVEN

CRITICAL THINKING EXERCISES

1. Have you ever been nervous about plagiarism? Discuss a previous experience that you or a friend may have had concerning plagiarism and/or citation. What aspects of plagiarism and citation concern you the most? Are there areas that are not clear, or are you very confident in your skills and experience? Explain.

2. Practice paraphrasing and summarizing information from your sources. Remember that paraphrasing means you use your own words to express an author's idea, often in order to simplify or make it more understandable. Summarizing means you use your own words to provide a brief overview of the author's broad ideas and main points. Be sure to use the appropriate in-text citation method to note where you got the idea from. Need help? Use an online resource like Purdue OWL, Citation Fox, Google Scholar, or the appropriate style manual (APA, MLA, Chicago, etc.).

3. Using the appropriate style guide or online tutorial, create full citations for some or all of your sources. (Don't use an automatic citation generator on this part.) Now try using the citation generator in your database, catalog, or other online tool (EasyBib or Son of Citation Machine) to create citations for the same sources. Do the citations match exactly? Remember that punctuation, capitalization, and italicization are all important and differ across styles. Which option do you think is the most useful and effective for creating **CORRECT** citations and why?

4. Review the various Creative Commons licenses (http://creativecommons.org/licenses/). Why do you think there are so many options for creators? What advantages/disadvantages does each license have for the creator and those who use the work? How do these options differ from traditional copyright? Assign a Creative Commons license to your website/blog, if appropriate.

5. Review your blog/website/etc., and summarize your understanding of information literacy. How has your understanding changed from your first posts to now? How has your own past ignorance of information literacy affected the quality of your academic work? How will your current knowledge improve it? How do you plan on contributing to scholarly conversations, no matter how small? If you have a friend who also has an information literacy site, review their postings and see how their viewpoints and understanding compare to your own. If you had to teach information literacy concepts to someone else, what would you emphasize and why?

CONCLUSION

ACKNOWLEDGMENTS

This book has been a frustrating and wonderful endeavor. Our efforts could and did falter along the way, but we were able to make it to the end thanks to the support of our editor, David Morrow. His professionalism, encouragement, and willingness to take on an unusual project continually improved our own work and expectations. Thank you, David.

We would also like to thank the many librarians who have shared their ideas, concerns, and excitement with us, directly and indirectly. The book was much improved, thanks to your input, even when we didn't want to hear it.

Matt thanks:

Irene, for her love, support, and ability to put up with my nonsense ALL THE TIME.

Colin, for his complete lack of concern about this project
and a steadfast focus on toy trains and playtime.

The upcoming yet-to-be-named baby, because I don't want your older
brother to brag about how he was thanked in a comic and you weren't.

My mom and dad, for raising a kid who hid in the corner of the library
reading about alien abductions and did a research poster presentation
on the JFK assassination in fourth grade. What a weirdo.

Each and every one of my old colleagues at Emporia State
University, who always encouraged me to keep running with these
goofy ideas, especially John Sheridan and Dale Monobe.

Mike, for being a great collaborator and friend. Thanks for getting me back into comics.

Kevin, for stepping in and making library research skills fun to look at.

Am I allowed to thank Batman? That seems gratuitous,
and he really didn't help that much.

Mike thanks:

My wife, Lily, for being generally awesome (and remarkably
understanding of my mountains of books, toys, and comics).

Jack Kirby, for the decades of inspiration.

Matt, for steering me into libraries as a profession, being my friend
despite my mercurial temperament, and introducing me to my wife.

Kevin thanks:

Matt and David, for bringing me into such an entertaining project.

The editing, design, and production staff at the University of
Chicago Press, for making this book such a joy to work on.

We are also specifically indebted to the work of the following groups and individuals. Their efforts informed this book in numerous ways, but were especially useful in encouraging a shift toward a more "holistic" approach to teaching and assessing information literacy and helped make this book way more interesting than it would have been otherwise.

The ACRL Information Literacy Competency Standards for Higher Education
Task Force for their ongoing revision of the *Framework for Information
Literacy for Higher Education* (http://acrl.ala.org/ilstandards/).

Korey Brunetti, Amy R. Hofer, and Lori Townsend for their work on threshold concepts and information literacy. See their work at http://www.ilthresholdconcepts.com/.

Trudi Jacobson and Thomas P. Mackey for their work on
metaliteracy. See their work at http://metaliteracy.org/.

Librarians at California State University, Chico, for coming up with the CRAAP
test, an excellent set of criteria for evaluating information. View the CRAAP test
in all its glory at http://www.csuchico.edu/lins/handouts/eval_websites.pdf.

GLOSSARY

advanced searching. Many catalogs, databases, and search engines offer advanced search options that allow you to make searching more effective and precise. These options, which can vary by resource, might allow you to choose to search by keyword, subject, author, title, document type, etc. You may also be able to add in Boolean operators (**AND**, **OR**, **NOT**) using a drop-down menu within an advanced search.

author search. A type of advanced search that allows you to search for resources by the name of the author. Traditionally, it is best to perform an author search by listing the last name of the author followed by a comma and then the author's first name, if necessary, although the comma is increasingly unnecessary in more and more library resources. Example: Smith, Earl

bibliography. May also be known as a works cited or reference list (although they are technically different, they essentially serve the same purpose), depending on the writing style you are using (APA, MLA, and Chicago are common examples of style). Basically, a bibliography lists the sources that an author has utilized in the research and writing of a paper, article, or book. This list provides a way for others to find, examine, and verify the information that was used in the research. A good existing bibliography can also help you get your own research started, as well. If you find a good source, check their bibliography for other potential sources for your own research.

Boolean operators. AND, **OR**, and **NOT** are known as Boolean operators within online library catalogs, databases, and search engines. You can use these terms to "connect" your search terms and appropriately narrow or broaden your search for information. **AND** can be used to narrow a search. For example, a search for "obesity **AND** children" would help you find materials that address both of those terms. **OR** is used to broaden a search and is useful for when you are dealing with terms that might be interchangeable. A good example of this is a search for "teens **OR** adolescents." **NOT** is used to limit a search by eliminating a specific term from your results. You could use a search for "immigration law **NOT** United States" to help you find information on immigration law outside the United States. You can also use multiple operators within a search, either within the search bar using parentheses or with advanced searching options. A more complex search might look like this: "(birth control **OR** contraception) **AND** (United States **OR** Europe)."

catalog. A library catalog is a tool that can be used to locate both physical materials (like books, journals, and DVDs) within a library and digital items (such as e-books) that have been made available as part of a library's resources. Many catalogs will allow you to find journals and other periodicals, but will not allow you to search within them for specific articles. This is changing with the increased use of tools called **Discovery Services.**

citation. The process of explaining where you found the information you're using in your re search. This includes the use of in-text citations, footnotes, or endnotes to indicate when you've used information from a specific source, as well as the full reference included in the bibliography/works cited/reference list that notes details such as the author, title, date, and other identifying information for a source.

citation styles. Various organizations have developed particular writing styles for different academic disciplines and purposes. Common examples of styles are APA (American Psychological Association), MLA (Modern Language Association), and Chicago style. These styles differ in many aspects, but one of the most obvious and important ways is how sources are cited. Although the information included in the citations can be very similar, the order of the information, as well as punctuation, capitalization, and the actual in-text citation/footnote/endnote will vary. For more information, check your appropriate style manual or use a reliable online resource like Purdue's Online Writing Lab (OWL).

classification. Refers to the various systems used to organize and locate information within a library. Common systems used in the United States include the Dewey Decimal system and the Library of Congress system. Essentially, classification helps keep similar items grouped together, which can allow for more efficient access to materials. These two systems break down information into broad subjects, with more and more narrow ranges of information fitting in within each broad range. Items are often assigned a call number based on where they fall within the classification system. These call numbers are used to place items in a specific order so that they can be located later, usually by locating the call number within the library **catalog**.

controlled vocabulary. A way to provide a standardized and single term that can be used in the place of similar terms, especially in the case of library catalogs and databases. For example, the term "automobile" may be used in the place of car, truck, van, etc. Controlled vocabularies make searching a less chaotic process by assigning identical terms to resources that cover similar material. **Subject headings** are a type of controlled vocabulary.

database. Simply put, a database is a collection of information that is organized and searchable. One type of database is a library **catalog**, which lets you search through materials in the library. Generally, though, when you hear the term "database," it refers to a library resource that can be used to locate digital articles from academic journals, newspapers, magazines, and other resources. Databases, unlike many catalogs, let you search within a journal title for a specific article.

Dewey Decimal classification. *See* **classification.**

Discovery Service (catalog/tool). Discovery Services are relatively new tools that libraries can use (in theory) to create a more streamlined search process for you, the student. These tools allow you to do one search for materials across multiple resources (catalogs and databases) instead of many searches. This can potentially save you time, but since there are multiple systems involved, things might slip through the cracks, as well.

faceted searching. This is a way to refine or limit your list of search results, much like you can do when shopping online. For example, you might be searching for a tent to purchase. You search the store for "tent" and then notice that you can narrow your search by the brand or capacity. You can often find the same kind of tools within a library catalog or database, except you can limit your search results by subject, format, location, date of publication, and many other variables. This approach lets you have the freedom of entering your own search terms and then narrowing down your results in a very controlled manner.

Google. Just Google it.

information overload. We all deal with an insane amount of information. Sometimes it can be too difficult to manage, especially when you are trying to do research and just don't know how to find the right information floating out there in the middle of all the wrong information. That's information overload, and you can help prevent it by knowing how to best utilize library and web resources, as well as understanding how to evaluate and use the information that you are able to locate through those resources.

journals (academic/peer-reviewed/scholarly). Academic journals are periodical publications that can be found in print or online and offer the most up-to-date research on a given topic. They're like magazines written by and for professors and researchers. Research is usually reviewed by other professionals before it is published to make sure the information is correct (*see* **peer review**). There are thousands and thousands of journals out there, so there are probably many that address your research topic. Typically, your best bet for accessing journals in your library is through a database, although many libraries still carry hard copies.

keyword searching. Usually, the generic default search option in a library catalog or database. Keywords can be potentially be found anywhere in a **record** or the full-text of an item, so this type of search may not be very useful unless you use multiple keywords connected with **Boolean operators.**

Library of Congress classification. *See* **classification.**

metadata. When discussing library tools like databases and catalogs, metadata can be understood as descriptive information about the items within those databases and catalogs. Metadata might describe the author, title, subject, and contents of a book, as well as its physical dimensions, call number, format type, and many other traits. Although the actual metadata **record** looks complicated, it is presented to you, the library patron, in a very simple format. When you view the details of an item in a database or catalog, you are viewing a "cleaned-up" version of the metadata. Metadata makes searching easier by providing a structure to the way that the descriptive information is recorded, organized, and searched. When you perform a search, it is the metadata that is being examined.

peer review. This refers to the process that academic/scholarly journal articles (and other publications) go through to help ensure that the research is accurate, reliable, and up-to-date before it is published. Basically, an author submits their article to a journal where an editor decides if the article will be considered for publication. If so, the article is sent out to be read and reviewed by other professionals in the field who help determine if the work is accurate and if it makes a new contribution to existing research on that topic. The reviewers may suggest edits and the author will consider revising the article before the editor makes a final decision on whether to publish it or not.

periodicals. Unlike books, periodicals (like newspapers, magazines, and academic journals) are continually published on a schedule (daily, weekly, monthly, etc.) with new content in every "issue." The traditional idea of periodicals is changing with technology. Websites can update information on a minute-to-minute basis without having to worry about publishing a physical item. Still, even though many academic journals and popular periodicals can use the Web to stay current and offer updates, they may continue to release articles and other materials that require review or editing on a scheduled basis. More and more often, you will be likely to access periodical articles (especially from academic journals) through your library **databases** or **Discovery Service.**

record. When using a catalog or database, the record refers to the information that describes the item or resource. You usually encounter a record after you click on a link to a specific item in the database or catalog. The record includes information like author, title, publisher, subject headings, contents, and call number, journal title, volume and issue (if applicable). This information is part of the **metadata** that is used to describe the item.

reference list. *See* **bibliography.**

research. Refers to the process of developing a research topic, establishing a question or a thesis statement, and then collecting appropriate information from various resources in order to address that question. It is about knowing how to locate the right information using the right tools in the right way. Remember that there are different types of research. Library research doesn't require you to wear a lab coat and laugh maniacally, although that might help to clear a study space in the library.

search engine. Google, Yahoo, and Bing are all examples of popular search engines that are used to search the Web for information. Search engines work by using "spiders" or "crawlers" to head out into the Web and bring back information from all the websites they can visit. Copies of web pages are stored by each search engine and are combed through when you perform a search. Remember that each search engine is different and may give you different results for identical searches. Search engines have advanced search options, but they differ somewhat from those found in catalogs and databases since the **metadata** for websites is different than for library resources.

search statement. When searching in a library **catalog** or **database** or when using a web **search engine**, a search statement refers to what you put in the search bar. It is best to create a search statement using good terms or **keywords** drawn from your research question or topic and connect them with **Boolean operators** to ensure good search results. For example, if your topic was the effects of pets on elderly health, your search statement might be "pets **AND** elderly **AND** health" or maybe just "pets **AND** elderly." You want to make sure that you eliminate the "fluff" from your search statements and include the essential terms.

search terms. *See* **search statement.**

spiders/crawlers. *See* **search engine.**

subject headings/subject terms. These are a type of **controlled vocabulary** used to describe what a resource is about. Subject terms are more specific than **keywords** since a keyword can be found anywhere within a record. A subject term or heading is a specific part of the **metadata** and can be searched separately (much like a title or an author search). In many catalogs and databases, a subject search (a type of **advanced searching** technique) will not result in a list of items, but a list of relevant subjects and subdivisions that can then be used to locate items that fit that specific subject heading. For example, I might perform a subject search in a database for "environmental policy." The list might give me a broad subject heading for "environmental policy" that would result in many articles on the subject, but I could also look at the subdivisions for the subject and notice that there are options for looking at resources on the health and ethical aspects of environmental policy. The number of articles under those specific subheadings would be narrower and perhaps more appropriate to my topic.

subject searching. *See* **subject headings.**

title search. An **advanced search** option used to search for items by their title. A title search specifically looks at the part of the **metadata** record that deals with the title of the item.

truncation. *See* **wildcard.**

Wikipedia. A web encyclopedia that can potentially be edited by anyone. *Wikipedia* can be an excellent starting point for your research and can help you get a very basic idea of a topic, as well as guide you toward other, more scholarly resources. Remember that the information from a *Wikipedia* article came from somewhere, so you should go to the original source if you want to use the information in your own research. It's not generally advisable to use and cite *Wikipedia* in your academic research, unless of course, you are researching *Wikipedia*!

wildcard. An **advanced search** option used to help you find resources that may use multiple spellings or variations. Catalogs and databases often offer multiple wildcard options, sometimes allowing a special character to stand in for other characters. Truncation is an example of a wildcard option. Although each database or catalog may use a different symbol to indicate truncation, an asterisk is often used. Example: a search for "theor*" would result in resources including "theory," "theoretical," "theorist," etc.

works cited. *See* **bibliography.**